**New Directions for
Community Colleges**

Arthur M. Cohen
EDITOR-IN-CHIEF

Richard L. Wagoner
ASSOCIATE EDITOR

Gabriel Jones
MANAGING EDITOR

D1104486

Hiring the Next Generation of Faculty

Brent D. Cejda
John P. Murray
EDITORS

Number 152 • Winter 2010
Jossey-Bass
San Francisco

Hiring the Next Generation of Faculty
Brent D. Cejda, John P. Murray (eds.)
New Directions for Community Colleges, no. 152

Arthur M. Cohen, Editor-in-Chief
Richard L. Wagoner, Associate Editor
Gabriel Jones, Managing Editor

NEW DIRECTIONS FOR COMMUNITY COLLEGES (ISSN 0194-3081, electronic ISSN 1536-0733) is part of The Jossey-Bass Higher and Adult Education Series and is published quarterly by Wiley Subscription Services, Inc., A Wiley Company, at Jossey-Bass, 989 Market Street, San Francisco, CA 94103-1741. Periodicals Postage Paid at San Francisco, California, and at additional mailing offices. POSTMASTER: Send address changes to New Directions for Community Colleges, Jossey-Bass, 989 Market Street, San Francisco, CA 94103-1741.

SUBSCRIPTIONS cost $89.00 for individuals and $259.00 for institutions, agencies, and libraries in the United States. Prices subject to change.

EDITORIAL CORRESPONDENCE should be sent to the Editor-in-Chief, Arthur M. Cohen, at the Graduate School of Education and Information Studies, University of California, Box 951521, Los Angeles, CA 90095-1521. All manuscripts receive anonymous reviews by external referees.

New Directions for Community Colleges is indexed in CIJE: Current Index to Journals in Education (ERIC), Contents Pages in Education (T&F), Current Abstracts (EBSCO), Ed/Net (Simpson Communications), Education Index/Abstracts (H. W. Wilson), Educational Research Abstracts Online (T&F), ERIC Database (Education Resources Information Center), and Resources in Education (ERIC).

Microfilm copies of issues and articles are available in 16mm and 35mm, as well as microfiche in 105mm, through University Microfilms Inc., 300 North Zeeb Road, Ann Arbor, MI 48106-1346.

CONTENTS

Editors' Notes

Because of past hiring patterns, some researchers are predicting that between 40 and 80 percent of community college faculty members may retire by 2015. Although such prophecies are often confounded by unanticipated external events (such as a financial crisis affecting retirement accounts), the evidence is that a large number of retirements are coming. Hiring decisions are likely to be the most important decisions community college leaders will make in their entire careers. Not only are they likely to be investing $3 million investment in each new employee to support salary and faculty support and development (Hammons cited by Flannigan, Jones, and Moore, 2004), but they are also shaping the future of the community college movement.

Where will community colleges leaders find these new faculty? It does not appear that many college students aspire to a career teaching in a community college (Evelyn, 2001; Murray and Cunningham, 2004). Nor does it appear that they will come from graduate schools. An ample literature suggests that students completing graduate degrees are poorly prepared by their graduate schools to assume the roles as faculty members, particularly at institutions that emphasize teaching over research (Grubb, 1999; Murray, 2005; Murray and Cunningham, 2004; Meacham, 2003; Tierney and Rhoads, 1994).

Community college leaders are facing the daunting challenge of replacing the faculty who in many ways shaped the colleges into what they are today. These leaders will need to seek individuals who understand and accept the democratic and egalitarian mission of community colleges. If community colleges are to continue to be "people's colleges," we must seek "talented, community college-minded faculty [who are] adequately prepared to address the needs of an increasingly diverse student population" (Gibson-Harman, Rodriguez, and Haworth, 2002, pp. 2–3). Yet at the same time, community colleges have an opportunity to shape their future in ways hitherto nearly impossible. As older faculty leave, the door opens to advances in curriculum, pedagogy, and course delivery methods for new curricula that may better meet the needs of students today.

Community college leaders need to carefully consider what ought to be their future missions and who will best help them shape this future. It is the contention of this volume that the hiring, socialization, and retention of new faculty members will rank high among the most important tasks facing today's leaders and will in a large way be their legacy.

New Directions for Community Colleges, no. 152, Winter 2010 © 2010 Wiley Periodicals, Inc.
Published online in Wiley Online Library (wileyonlinelibrary.com) • DOI: 10.1002/cc.421

The primary audiences for this volume of *New Directions for Community Colleges* are administrators and faculty working in community colleges who will lead the efforts to recruit and hire the next generation of faculty members. Government officials and policymakers who are responsible for promoting the community college as the primary institution for workforce training and development should also find this volume of interest as they consider funding implications in a time of scarce resources. University educators and researchers will benefit from these chapters, which add to the existing research base for community colleges and suggest a number of areas for future exploration.

To set the stage for this volume, Chapter One by John Murray examines the scope and causes of the problem. He also discusses considerations that should be taken into account when hiring faculty to teach in the community college environment, arguing that candidates must be committed to the teaching mission of the community college. In Chapter Two, Pamela Eddy notes that faculty members come to the community college through a variety of routes, most often not as an intended career option. She discusses how their socialization in graduate school and in other careers affects the issues faculty face as they start their careers. Eddy points out that faculty members working in urban settings face different challenges relative to their counterparts in rural locations. In addition, size differences in student enrollment affect the faculty experience. Next, Mary Bendickson and Karen Griffin describe Hillsborough Community College's unique program for socializing faculty who are new to the community college environment. They describe and evaluate its forty-five-hour orientation program for new faculty and offer suggestions for other community college administrators who might wish to adopt the program.

The next three chapters offer perspectives from a specific institutional type and from specific faculty characteristics. Brent Cejda notes in Chapter Four that 57 percent of public community colleges in the 2005 Carnegie classifications of colleges are classified as rural and documents that the unique characteristics of these colleges present challenges to the recruitment of a qualified pool of faculty. He discusses as well factors related to the socialization of faculty into the rural community college environment, an essential component to retention. He ends with recommendations for policy and practice. In Chapter Five, Jaime Lester and Trudy Bers explore the attractiveness of community colleges for female faculty. Using a review of the literature on female faculty in community colleges, the authors highlight several areas—feminization of academic disciplines, work-life balance, interpersonal gender dynamics—that need continued improvement to attract and retain female faculty. They offer specific recommendations for changes to policies and practices. In Chapter Six, William Vega, Kenneth Yglesias, and John Murray explore the need to diversify the faculty and point out the importance of mentoring minority faculty members. In their view, a robust and informed mentoring system is necessary to ensure the success and retention of qualified faculty.

The final three chapters are directed to the community college administrators who face the challenge of filling numerous upcoming faculty vacancies. In Chapter Seven, Roy Rodriguez provides a thorough review of recent court decisions regarding hiring, evaluating, and dismissing community college employees. He explores how the increasing reliance on adjunct faculty might affect contracts and policy and how the courts might interpret such documents. In Chapter Eight, Marie Foster Gnage and Kevin Drumm argue that hiring employees who are committed to student success is critical to the mission of community colleges. Instructional leaders must ensure that the hiring process reflects the desired outcome by first defining student success and then allowing the definition and description to guide all steps of the hiring process. In the final chapter, community college administrators Donald Green and Kathleen Ciez-Volz point out the importance of honoring the past in the transition into the future. They provide a practitioner's view of the qualities of exemplary teachers and offer recommendations for increasing the effectiveness and efficiency of faculty hiring processes.

Brent D. Cejda
John P. Murray
Editors

References

Burke, J. C. "Graduate Schools Should Require Internships for Teaching." *The Chronicle Review,* October 5, 2001, p. B6.

Clarke, B. "Small Worlds, Different Worlds: The Uniqueness and Troubles of American Academic Professions." *Daedalus,* Fall 1997, *126*(4), 21–42.

Evelyn, J. "Community Colleges Face a Crisis of Leadership." *Chronicle of Higher Education,* 2001, pp. 36–37.

Flannigan, S., Jones, B. R., and Moore Jr., W. "An Exploration of Faculty Hiring Practices in Community Colleges." *Community College Journal of Research and Practice,* 2004, *28*(10), 823–836.

Gibson-Harman, K., Rodriguez, S., and Haworth, J. G. "Community College Faculty and Professional Staff: The Human Resource Challenge." In T. Bers and H. D. Calhoun (eds.), *Next Steps for the Community College.* New Directions for Community Colleges, no. 117. San Francisco: Jossey-Bass, 2002.

Grubb, N. W. *Honored But Invisible: An Inside Look at Teaching in Community Colleges.* New York: Routledge, 1999.

Meacham, J. "Our Doctoral Programs Are Failing Our Undergraduate Students." *Liberal Education,* 2003, *89*(3), 22–27.

Murray, J. P. "Meeting the Needs of New Faculty at Rural Community Colleges." *Community College Journal of Research and Practice,* 2005, *29*(3), 215–232.

Murray, J. P., and Cunningham, S. "New Community College Faculty Members and Job Satisfaction." *Community College Review,* 2004, *32*(2), 19–32.

Tierney, W. G., and Rhoads, R. A. *Faculty Socialization as Cultural Process: A Mirror of Institutional Commitment*. ASHE-ERIC Higher Education Report, no. 93–6. Hoboken, N.J.: Wiley, 1994.

BRENT D. CEJDA *is associate professor in the Department of Educational Administration at the University of Nebraska–Lincoln and executive director of the National Council of Instructional Administrators.*

JOHN P. MURRAY *is a professor in the Department of Advanced Studies in Education and Counseling, California State University, Long Beach.*

NEW DIRECTIONS FOR COMMUNITY COLLEGES • DOI: 10.1002/cc

1

*Community colleges are facing difficult times. Resources
are becoming increasingly scarce, enrollments are growing
to unprecedented numbers, the student body is becoming
increasingly diverse, the economic downturn continues to
have an effect on curriculum and mission, increased
demands for accountability are driving decisions, and
faculty turnover is rapidly becoming a problem as baby
boomers retire.*

Preparing to Hire the Best in the Perfect Storm

John P. Murray

From a casual glance at the literature on community college faculty, it
appears to have been taken for granted that large numbers of full-time community college faculty will be retiring in the near future. Although such
predictions are often confounded by external events that the forecasters
had not anticipated (such as a financial crisis affecting retirement accounts),
there is evidence that a large number of retirements are coming sooner or
later and that community colleges need to plan to replace exiting faculty.
This may turn out to be a bigger task than many community college leaders
have anticipated. Because of past hiring patterns, some researchers are predicting community colleges may have 40 to 80 percent of their faculty
members retire by 2015 (Finkel, 2005; Fugate and Amey, 2000; Gahn and
Twombly, 2001; Gibson-Harman, Rodriguez, and Haworth, 2002; Rifkin,
2000; Townsend and Twombly, 2007). Assuming that many of the newly
hired faculty will stay with the same college for twenty-five to thirty years,
as have their predecessors, this anticipated wave of hiring decisions is likely
to be the most important decisions that community college leaders will
make in their entire careers.

According to the 2008 *Chronicle of Higher Education Almanac,* public
community colleges employ 354,497 full-time community college faculty
members. Of these, 29.2 percent are younger than forty-five years of age,
34.4 percent are between forty-five and fifty-four years old, 31.7 percent are
between fifty-five and sixty-four years old, and 4.7 percent are sixty-five

New Directions for Community Colleges, no. 152, Winter 2010 © 2010 Wiley Periodicals, Inc.
Published online in Wiley Online Library (wileyonlinelibrary.com) • DOI: 10.1002/cc.422

or older. Public community colleges have a larger percentage of faculty between the ages of forty-five and sixty-four (66.1 percent) and the lowest percentage of faculty sixty-five or older than any other segment of higher education. This would suggest that community college faculty tend to retire at or near the traditional retirement age of sixty-five. Gahn and Twombly (2001) found that community college faculty anticipate retiring at 61.5 years. Using statistics from the 2004 National Study of Postsecondary Faculty conducted by the National Center for Education Statistics, O'Banion (2006–2007) calculated that public community colleges will need to replace approximately 18,375 full-time faculty members in the next ten years. Moreover, there are indications that many community college faculty members will take early retirement if it were offered to them. Hardy and Santos Laanan (2006) found than 57 percent of the community college faculty they sampled would consider early retirement. Gahn and Twombly (2001) noted that community college faculty with twenty or more years of service indicated that they were "somewhat" or "very likely" to retire within three years.

Faculty in some disciplines and regions of the country may already be experiencing high rates of retirements. In 2001, a national study found that 27 percent of current full-time faculty members in the areas of general education and transfer, business, and developmental education were fifty-five years old or older (Berry, Hammons, and Denny, 2001). Hardy and Santos Laanan (2006) reported that "with over 60 percent of their faculty over the age of 55 (and 42 percent over the age of 65) in 1999, those institutions in the Far West (i.e., California, Oregon, and Washington) stand to feel the impact of these changes first. The Southeast region of the United States is similarly positioned for a major wave of retirement and replacement, with 45 percent of the faculty in this region being age 55 or above" (p. 808). In a single college district (Pima Community College, in Arizona) 54.7 percent of its full-time faculty is eligible to retire now, and the district anticipates that by 2010, 67.2 percent of its faculty will be eligible to take advantage of the state's retirement benefits (McCormack, 2008).

At the same time faculty are leaving, students are enrolling in greater numbers than ever before. All sectors of higher education are reporting enrollment increases. The National Center for Education Statistics (2005) predicts that college enrollments will increase between 9 and 16 percent (or between 9.4 and 20.6 million new students) by 2017. Assuming that past enrollment patterns hold true for future enrollments, nearly half of these future students will enroll in community colleges.

In fact, there are strong indications that community college enrollments may grow faster than other segments of higher education. The recent economic downturn has caused many unemployed individuals to seek additional skills or new careers ("Community College Enrollment Rises as Economic Angst Grows"; "Nevada Two-Year College Enrollments Spike Due to Faltering Economy," 2009). Moreover, families have become more cost-conscious as tuition rises in a time of economic turmoil, and parents are encouraging their children to gain their first two years of college at less-expensive community colleges ("As Economy Sags Enrollment Surges at Community Colleges," 2008). Even if the trend toward increased reliance on adjunct faculty continues, "community colleges face a demand for faculty not seen since the community college growth spurt of the 1960s and 1970s" (Twombly, 2005, p. 424).

Threat or Opportunity

The loss of the faculty who built community colleges into what they are today is both a serious threat to community colleges and an opportunity:

> The challenges are to attract sufficient numbers of qualified new faculty in community colleges to replace those who are leaving and to ensure those who are employed understand and are committed to the community college mission and values. However, turnover also provides an opportunity to bring new energy and greater diversity into the movement [Boggs, 2008, p. vii].

Community colleges are caught in a double bind: retirements are creating vacancies at a time when resources are shrinking and enrollments and costs are increasing. Replacing retiring faculty becomes much more difficult than in the past, and many full-time positions may be left unfilled. However, at some point, colleges will have to hire full-time faculty. Because of dwindling resources, these colleges may not be able to replace every departing faculty member; it therefore becomes paramount to carefully consider the long-term needs of the college.

With each new faculty hired, community college leaders have the unique opportunity to shape the future of the college. However, this opportunity also places a tremendous responsibility in the hands of these leaders. Community college leaders face the intimidating challenge of replacing the faculty who in many ways shaped the colleges into what they are today. The leaders will need to seek individuals who understand and accept the community college's democratic and egalitarian mission. If the community college is to continue to be the "people's college," leaders must seek "talented, community-college-minded faculty [who are] adequately prepared to address the needs of an increasingly diverse student population" (Gibson-Harman, Rodriguez, and Haworth, 2002, pp. 2–3).

At the same time, community colleges have an opportunity to shape their future in ways that thus far have been nearly impossible. As older faculty leave, they open the door to advances in curriculum, pedagogy, and course delivery methods. This makes it imperative that community college leaders carefully consider what ought to be their future missions and who will best help them shape this future. It is the contention of this volume that the hiring, socialization, and retention of new faculty members will rank high among the most important tasks facing today's leaders and will in a large way be their legacy.

Community colleges cannot afford to hire anyone simply because he or she meets minimum qualifications. Around 72 percent of community colleges offer tenure (Twombly and Townsend, 2008), raising the prospect of a thirty-year career at a single institution, which according to Hammons represents a $3 million investment (as cited by Flannigan, Jones, and Moore, 2004). Community college leaders have at least two overlapping considerations when recruiting and hiring faculty: First, community colleges take enormous pride in placing teaching at the heart of their mission; and second, these colleges are strongly committed to an open-door philosophy that welcomes all. Consequently, faculty must be committed to and able to teach an extremely diverse student body.

Prospective community college faculty must be willing and able to deal with heavier teaching loads than at other institutions and with more diverse student bodies (Townsend and Twombly, 2007). These student bodies often include adult, commuting, part-time, and academically underprepared students who have family and work commitments in addition to their studies. Consequently, community colleges are "much more interested in people [students] who will fit in with our college's community" (Evelyn, 2001, p. A8).

Where will community colleges leaders find these new faculty members? According to Jones-Kavalier and Flannigan (2008), community college leaders express concern "that there are not enough qualified, passionate, and committed people who are willing to apply for full-time positions" (p. 122). Often college students and graduates are either unaware of (Evelyn, 2001; Fugate and Amey, 2000; Murray and Cunningham, 2004) or uninterested (Shoup and Keeler, 2009; Twombly and Townsend, 2008; Winter and Kjorlien, 2000) in a community college teaching career. In a survey of over four thousand doctoral students, Golde and Dore (2001) found that only 3.9 percent aspired to a community college teaching position; 16.6 percent, however, believed that such a career was their likely fate.

Moreover, it does not appear that graduate schools are preparing individuals to teach in community colleges. An ample literature suggests that students completing graduate degrees are poorly prepared by their graduate schools to assume the role of faculty member, particularly at institutions that emphasize teaching over research. Research universities prepare researchers. "A serious problem may result when a new faculty member oriented toward a disciplinary culture of research is hired at a teaching-oriented institution" (Tierney and Rhoads, 1994, p. 34). Often there is a profound disconnect between what research universities address in educating the next generation of faculty members and what most in the higher education community want in order to fulfill their missions: "Most doctoral programs and faculty would not acknowledge, much less assume, responsibility for ensuring that their graduates have any of the qualities that community, liberal arts, and master's campuses are seeking. Most would not know how to be good teachers for the students in a community or liberal arts college environment. To ask doctoral faculty at research universities to prepare their students to be effective teachers would be to ask for what most are not able to do" (Meacham, 2003, p. 25).

Even if faculty were better prepared for the realities of employment at nonresearch universities, many are unacquainted with the challenges of teaching in an open-door institution (Watts and Hammons, 2002). When novice community college faculty are interviewed, they say that the most frequent causes of dissatisfaction stem from a failure to understand the diversity of the community college student body, the intense workload, and the emphasis that community colleges place on teaching and learning (Murray, 2005; Murray and Cunningham, 2004). Grubb points (1999) out:

> The most basic fact of instructors' lives is that, if they are conscientious, they are overloaded. The typical teaching load is five classes, which usually meet three hours per week, and somewhat more for occupational instructors. Institutions make their money on enrollments. Therefore, many instructors face between 25 and 35 students per class, or perhaps 150 students at a time; grading the frequent quizzes and papers therefore adds considerably to the fifteen to twenty hours per week of contact time. Full-time faculty are also responsible for institutional maintenance; in a period when the numbers of part-time faculty have been increasing, the price of being a full-time instructor is having to supervise part-time instructors and carry out administrative chores [pp. 281–282].

Identifying the Best

Community colleges often lack a clear idea of what they want in a faculty member. They usually rely on generic job descriptions that tend to use "nebulous, ambiguous and deliberately vague terms" ("The Perils of 'Fit,'" 2009) that focus on the minimum requirements (Townsend and Twombly, 2007). However, experience shows that although possessing minimum requirements may be a necessary requirement to satisfy regional accrediting agencies, the mere possession of the minimal requirements is hardly a sufficient condition to be a successful faculty member. The required qualifications most often address the appropriate academic credential and minimal experience in teaching or, in the case of vocational faculty, the appropriate work experience. Often teaching and work experience are judged in terms of years, and rarely do employment advertisements ask for proof of teaching ability (Grubb, 1999; Townsend and Twombly, 2007). When community colleges attempt to judge an applicant's teaching ability, it is most often based on a fifteen- to twenty-minute teaching demonstration given to faculty, not students. The deficiencies of recruiting may not be a serious concern because it appears that these employment ads do not seem to influence the quality of the pool (Grubb, 1999; Townsend and Twombly, 2007).

Not all newly hired faculty work out. In the early days of my career, a dean or department chair would often acknowledge the person's knowledge of the discipline and attribute the failure to the lack of "human relation skills." Today, failure is more likely to be attributed to lack of fit. I am not sure the explanation is any clearer, but I will acknowledge that person-environment fit plays a huge role in a person's success or failure at a particular organization. In a discussion of the difference between a successful and unsuccessful executive, Gorman and Hoopes (1999) write:

> Fit with the culture is more important than whether a candidate has the prerequisite experience, skills, and expertise to do the job. . . . what differentiated selecting successful executives from unsuccessful executives was not track record or technical expertise but fit issues, including fit to the boss, fit to the organizational culture, values, and interpersonal characteristics and style [p. 10].

I would argue that this is as true for faculty as for executives. The difficulty is determining what we mean by "fit." Unlike credentials and years of experience, fit is not quantifiable and therefore is susceptible to abuse. It can easily become a buzzword for arbitrary and unscrupulous judgments.

Despite the vagueness inherent in the concept, it is clear that person-environment fit is key to making good hiring decisions (Barden, 2007). However, hiring committees need to develop a shared concept of what is meant by a "good fit" at their institution. The question is how they do this. When we look to the theoretical literature, we find various similar definitions of *person-environment fit*. A good fit "results from the congruence between the demands of the organization and the abilities of the employee to meet those demands" (Westerman, 2001, p. 5). However, this tautology is of little help to a hiring committee struggling to match the right candidate to the institution.

How do committee members go about developing a useful definition of person-environment fit? According to O'Reilly, Chatman, and Caldwell (1991), developing an understanding of fit starts with an understanding of the organization's culture. Although these are often unique local circumstances (for example, a rural setting), some common elements of culture are found in all community colleges. The question then becomes:

> [Is] the person a good fit for the organization? [This] is sometimes the most difficult to determine; it is usually assessed by whether an individual's values seem consistent with those of the campus. In higher education, your institutional mission statement defines the school's shared values. If you are going to succeed in identifying the candidate who will fulfill your hiring priorities and, in turn, find fulfillment at your institution, you must revisit

that mission statement regularly and often throughout the search process [Van der Vorm, 2001].

Therefore, the first step in determining fit is an examination of the philosophical underpinnings of the community college mission. "Faculty work in community colleges is shaped by the institution's mission: its commitment to provide access to higher education to everyone who can benefit" (Twombly and Townsend, 2008, p. 14). Community colleges' commitment to open access results in a diverse student body. An instructor can have a class composed of recent high school graduates with varying levels of motivation, recently unemployed adults seeking a new career, immigrants and others for whom English is a second language, or senior citizens seeking personal enrichment. They will have come from several ethnic, cultural, and socioeconomic backgrounds and with academic abilities ranging from semiliterate to merit scholar. Prospective community college faculty should understand and accept that these differences are a consequence of the philosophical mission of the community college, or they will likely have unrealistic expectations.

It is the responsibility of the hiring committee to seek individuals who understand and accept the community college's democratic and egalitarian mission. If the college is to continue to be the "people's college," we must seek "talented, community-college-minded faculty [who are] adequately prepared to address the needs of an increasingly diverse student population" (Gibson-Harman, Rodriguez, and Haworth, 2002, pp. 2–3).

However, it is also critical that candidates be honest with themselves and assess the congruence between their values and those of the community college mission. Several researchers have found that community college faculty members who are committed to and accept the community college philosophy have more positive attitudes about their work and are often more effective teachers (DuBois, 1993; Harnish and Creamer, 1985–1986). However, a fifteen- to twenty-minute teaching demonstration and an hour-long interview are unlikely to provide the committee with an opportunity to evaluate a candidate's enthusiasm for the community college mission. Search committees "should decide what prospective faculty actually need to have experienced and learned to offer evidence that they both enjoy and value working with diverse students and are capable of building positive, cooperative relationships with them" (Higgins, Hawthorne, Cape, and Bell, 1994, p. 35).

Understanding and accepting the community college's democratic and egalitarian mission is a necessary but not sufficient condition. Prospective faculty members must also understand that teaching is the primary work of community college faculty. This means they must be prepared for heavy teaching loads. Most community college faculty teach five courses, which can mean two to five preparations a term and fifteen to twenty or more hours in the classroom every week. Huber (1998) found that community college faculty spend an average of 11.5 hours preparing for classes. Because typical class enrollments range from 20 to 35 students per section, an instructor can be responsible for 150 or more students a term. This often results in an oppressive number of quizzes, exams, and papers to grade without the assistance of a teaching assistant.

The heavy teaching load is often exacerbated because community college faculty by and large teach only introductory courses, which means that they teach the same four or five courses over and over for twenty to thirty years. The result can be stagnation and diminished job involvement (Altshuler and Richter, 1985; Harnish and Creamer, 1985–1986; Menges, 1984). Diligent faculty are often overwhelmed by the requirements of the job. As faculty become overloaded, their emphasis often shifts from pedagogical and student learning concerns to "simply surviving," limiting the chances of the community college to serve its wide variety of learners.

The diversity of the student body requires that faculty members understand and accept the special role of community colleges in the higher education hierarchy. They must be ready and willing to accept the challenges of the open door commitment by valuing every student. This means that hiring committees must search for the fit between the candidate and the college, and this means more than seeking the candidate who meets the minimum degree and years of experience.

Because hiring responsibly is a difficult task for most untrained and unprepared hiring committees, some refer to the process as a game. I would suggest, however, that it is much more serious than a gaming metaphor would suggest. A newly hired president, chancellor, vice president, or faculty member will affect the lives of many individuals. Moreover, the individuals affected may have tremendous impact on generations to come. When a faculty member tells a student that he or she is not college material, that student may leave college and start a life of low-paying jobs and periodic unemployment that can affect his or her family for generations. Stories abound about teachers who have influenced individual students to pursue higher aspirations than they originally thought possible. Hiring right is a difficult task and requires us to put forth our best efforts.

References

Altshuler, T. C., and Richter, S. L. "Maintaining Faculty Vitality." Edited by Donald E. Puyear and George B. Vaughan. New Directions for Community Colleges, no. 52. San Francisco: Jossey-Bass, 1985.

"As Economy Sags Enrollment Surges at Community Colleges." Community College Week, Sept. 2008. Retrieved November 1, 2010, from http://www.ccweek.com/news/templates/template.aspx?articleid=593&zoneid=3.

Barden, D. M. "A Fitting End." 2007. On Hiring. Retrieved June 25, 2007, from http://chronicle.com/article/A-Fitting-End/46587/.

Berry, L. H., Hammons, J. O., and Denny, G. S. "Faculty Retirement Turnover in Community Colleges: A Real or Imagined Problem?" Community College Journal of Research and Practice, 2001, 25, 123–136.

Boggs, G. R. "Foreword." In B. Jones-Kavalier and S. L. Flannigan (eds.), *The Hiring Game: Reshaping Community College Practice*. Washington, D.C.: Community College Press.

"Community College Enrollment Rises as Economic Angst Grows." *Community College Week*. Nov. 3, 2008. Retrieved November 1, 2010, from http://www.ccweek.com/news/templates/template.aspx?articleid=720&zoneid=3.

DuBois, G. "Hidden Characteristics of Effective Community College Teachers." *Community College Journal of Research and Practice*, 1993, *17*(5), 459–471.

Evelyn, J. "The Hiring Boom at Two-Year Colleges." *Chronicle of Higher Education*, June 15, 2001, pp. A8–A9.

Finkel, E. "The Calm Before the Storm." *Community College Week*, October 10, 2005, pp. 6–8.

Flannigan, S., Jones, B. R., and Moore, W. "An Exploration of Faculty Hiring Practices in Community Colleges." *Community College Journal of Research and Practice*, 2004, *28*, 823–836.

Fugate, A., and Amey, M. "Career Stages of Community College Faculty: A Qualitative Analysis of Their Career Paths, Roles, and Development." *Community College Review*, 2000, *28*(1), 1–22.

Gahn, S., and Twombly, S. "Dimensions of the Community College Faculty Labor Market." *Review of Higher Education*, 2001, *24*(3), 259–282.

Gibson-Harman, K., Rodriguez, S., and Haworth, J. G. "Community College Faculty and Professional Staff: The Human Resource Challenge." In T. Bers (ed.), *Next Steps for the Community College*. New Directions for Community Colleges, no. 117. San Francisco: Jossey-Bass, 2002.

Golde, C. M., and Dore, T. M. "At Cross-Purposes: What the Experiences of Today's Doctoral Students Reveal About Doctoral Education." 2001. Retrieved Oct. 6, 2009, from http://www.wcer.wisc.edu/phd-survey/golde.html.

Gorman, B., and Hoopes, L. "Hiring to Build Change Capacity: The Human Resource Role." *Human Resource Planning*, 1999, *22*(2), 8–10.

Grubb, N. W. *Honored But Invisible: An Inside Look at Teaching in Community Colleges*. New York: Routledge, 1999.

Hardy, D. E., and Santos Laanan, F. "Characteristics and Perspectives of Faculty at Public Two-Year Colleges." *Community College Journal of Research and Practice*, 2006, *30*, 787–811

Harnish, D., and Creamer, D. G. "Faculty Stagnation and Diminished Job Involvement." *Community College Review*, 1985–1986, *13*(3), 33–39.

Higgins, C. S., Hawthorne, E. M., Cape, J., and Bell, L. "The Successful Community College Instructor: A Profile for Recruitment." *Community College Review*, 1994, *21*(4), 27–36.

Huber, M. T. *Community College Faculty Attitudes and Trends, 1997*. Stanford, Calif.: National Center for Postsecondary Improvement, Stanford University, 1998.

Jones-Kavalier, B., and Flannigan, S. L. *The Hiring Game: Reshaping Community College Practice*. Washington, D.C.: Community College Press, 2008.

McCormack, E. "Community Colleges Hope to Keep Aging Professors in the Classroom." *Chronicle of Higher Education*, June 13, 2008, p. A14.

Meacham, J. "Our Doctoral Programs Are Failing Our Undergraduate Students." *Liberal Education*, 2003, *89*(3), 22–27.

Menges, R. J. "Career-Span Faculty Development." *College Teaching*, 1984, *33*(4), 181–184.

Murray, J. P. "Meeting the Needs of New Faculty at Rural Community Colleges." *Community College Journal of Research and Practice*, 2005, *29*(3), 215–232.

Murray, J. P., and Cunningham, S. "New Community College Faculty Members and Job Satisfaction." *Community College Review*, 2004, *32*(2), 19–39.

National Center for Education Statistics. *Projections of Education Statistics to 2017.* Washington, D.C.: National Center for Education Statistics, 2005. Retrieved Oct. 8, 2008, from http://nces.ed.gov/programs/digest/d05/tables/dt05_230.asp.

"Nevada Two Year College Enrollments Spike Due to Faltering Economy. *Community College Week,* January 25, 2009. Retrieved November 1, 2010 from http://www.ccweek.com/news/templates/template.aspx?articleid=892&zoneid=3.

O'Banion, T. "Crisis and Calamity in the Community College." *Community College Journal,* 2006–2007, 77(3), 44–47.

O'Reilly, C., Chatman, J., and Caldwell, D. "People and Organizational Culture: A Profile Comparison Approach to Assessing Person-Organization Fit." *Academy of Management Journal,* 1991, 14(2), 487–516.

"The Perils of 'Fit,' Part 2." *On Hiring,* Sept. 19, 2009. Retrieved Sept. 19, 2009, from http://chronicle.com/blogPost/The-Perils-of-Fit-Part-2/658/.

Rifkin, T. "Public Community College Faculty. New Expeditions: Charting the Second Century of Community College." Washington, D.C.: 2000. Community College Review.

Shoup, J., and Keeler, O. L. "Guarded Optimism for the Community College Staffing Pipeline." Paper presented at the American Educational Research Association (AERA) San Diego, Calif., 2009.

Tierney, W. G., and Rhoads, R. A. *Faculty Socialization as Cultural Process: A Mirror of Institutional Commitment.* ASHE-ERIC Higher Education Report, no. 93–6. Hoboken, N.J.: Wiley, 1994.

Townsend, B. K., and Twombly, S. B. *Community College Faculty: Overlooked and Undervalued.* ASHE-ERIC Higher Education Report, no. 32–6. Hoboken, N.J.: Wiley, 2007.

Twombly, S. "Values, Policies, and Practices Affecting the Hiring Process for Full-Time Arts and Sciences Faculty in Community Colleges." *Journal of Higher Education,* 2005, 76(4), 423–447.

Twombly, S., and Townsend, B. K. "Community College Faculty What We Know and Need to Know." *Community College Review,* 2008, 36(1), 5–24.

Van der Vorm, P. "The Well-Tempered Search: Hiring Faculty and Administrators for Mission." *Academe Onltne,* 2001, 87(3). Retrieved November 1, 2010 fromhttp://www.aaup.org/AAUP/pubsres/academe/2001/MJ/Feat/Vorm.htm.

Watts, G. E., and Hammons, J. O. "Professional Development: Setting and Context." *Enhancing Community Colleges Through Professional Development.* In G. E. Watts (ed.), New Directions for Community Colleges, no. 120. San Francisco: Jossey-Bass, 2002.

Westerman, J. *The Impact of Person-Organization Fit on Employee Attitudes and Outcomes.* New York: Edwin Mellen Press, 2001.

Winter, P. A., and Kjorlien, C. L. "Community College Faculty Recruitment: Predictors of Applicant Attraction to Faculty Positions." *Community College Review,* 2000, 28(1), 23–40.

JOHN P. MURRAY *is a professor in the Department of Advanced Studies in Education and Counseling, California State University, Long Beach.*

2

This chapter provides a portrait of faculty development in community colleges, highlighting different issues facing faculty based on location and including a review of the impact of socialization on how faculty approach their roles. Findings indicate that changing classrooms require a different type of faculty preparation and that links with regional universities are critical.

New Faculty Issues: Fitting In and Figuring It Out

Pamela L. Eddy

Faculty members come to the community college through a variety of routes, most often not as an intended career option (Fugate and Amey, 2000). Indeed, Townsend and Twombly (2007) underscore the varied pathways to faculty ranks at two-year colleges and point out that possession of a Ph.D. is gaining traction, but that the master's degree remains the coin of the realm for hiring in the sector. Coupled with the fact that recent research on faculty socialization (Austin, 2002; Eddy and Gaston-Gales, 2008) focuses on research university faculty versus those teaching at community colleges, community college search committees need to consider the match between candidate preparation and the skills required for successful classroom teaching. This chapter first highlights how previous socialization and preparation affect the issues faculty face as they start their careers and then discusses the areas faculty developers and academic leaders have indicated as pressing for faculty in community colleges. How faculty members were prepared, their previous experiences, and their expectations of teaching at a community college all contribute to how they conceptualize their faculty roles.

The location and focus of the two-year college also influences the experience of new faculty because context provides key environmental factors. Faculty members working in urban settings face different challenges relative to their counterparts in rural locations. In addition, size differences in student enrollment are important to the faculty experience. The research

New Directions for Community Colleges, no. 152, Winter 2010 © 2010 Wiley Periodicals, Inc.
Published online in Wiley Online Library (wileyonlinelibrary.com) • DOI: 10.1002/cc.423

reported in this chapter draws from two sources: data from a qualitative case study, which provides the underpinnings for understanding the impacts of how faculty prepared for their teaching positions, and data from a national study on faculty development, which highlights different faculty needs based on institutional size and location.

Socialization and Faculty Preparation

Faculty as adult learners approach their teaching based on various teaching perspectives (Pratt, 1998) and ingrained schemas (Harris, 1995; Weick, 1995). Underlying schemas provide a road map for adult learners on how to interpret new information based on past experience. Traditionally, graduate programs focused on disciplinary content issues versus socializing students for teaching roles (Austin, 2001). Therefore, new faculty most often learned how to teach by observation, trial and error, and reading on areas of interest. Townsend and Twombly's (2007) recent review of the literature regarding community college faculty points to differences relative to university faculty preparation and two-year college teachers, but they focus more on degree-level differences than variations in socialization for teaching roles. They also point out that the expected role of community college faculty is that of generalists rather than the specialist roles of their counterparts in university settings. These role differences ultimately point to diverse forms of socialization for teaching roles, with community college faculty work focused almost exclusively on teaching versus the work of university faculty members, who divide their attention between teaching and research.

Given the paucity of research on the socialization and career pathways of community college faculty, I have begun preliminary research into this topic. Data from a case study of faculty at a medium-size rural community college provide an inside look at the socialization process. Given the case nature of this research, generalities for all faculty are not possible, but common themes become evident. The diversity of community college settings means that the environment (urban, suburban, rural) and size (large, medium, small) have an impact on the lived experience of faculty life in a two-year college. Pointedly, the issues these faculty members face may differ based on context; for example, those in rural areas wear multiple hats and are fewer in number.

Participants for the research were selected based on their lead-faculty status. The college organizational chart did not have department chairs; thus, some of the functions typically assigned to that position were conducted by those designated as lead faculty for units. The rationale for this requirement included recognition of the small size of units that often resulted in there being only one full-time faculty member and a desire to obtain a longer period of work as a community college faculty. A longer time in the community college setting afforded participants a perspective on their experiences over the length of their career and experience in hiring other faculty and knowing more about the impact of preparation on induction in the teaching ranks. Semistructured interviews were conducted with six lead faculty. The format provided an opportunity for dialogue versus mere question and answer (Holstein and Gubrium, 1995; Ray, 1994). Data were analyzed using a framework for faculty socialization that focused on graduate programming socialization (Austin, 2001), sources of stress for new faculty (Sorcinelli, 2002), and challenges facing community college faculty (Eddy, 2005, 2007; Murray, 1999). Key findings from this research include a lack of intentional planning for a career as a community college faculty member, connections to the regional university, and links to practice.

Lack of Planning.   As the literature suggests (Fugate and Amey, 2000), faculty participants did not plan on teaching at a community college. Serendipity brought them to their current positions, but an underlying motivation revolved around the desire to focus on teaching. One of the participants noted that she did not complete college until she was an adult. She said, "I guess I was one of the students in high school that was convinced that you just didn't need to go to college to go anywhere in your career." Her career pathway started as an international flight attendant and included stints as a small travel business owner and trainer for Sylvan Learning Centers. She found she had a knack for training and a desire to get into higher education. Along the way, she acquired both a bachelor's degree and a master's degree. She was hired at the community college for a secretarial role but started to teach when a faculty position could not be filled. She was in the process of transitioning to a new position at a nearby university in its tourism department.

Two other faculty members noted that they initially had intended to go into high school teaching. The first recounted that "as part of the student-teaching process I decided that I wouldn't like working in the high school, so I was offered an assistantship and got my master's degree in English. I started working first in [a midwestern state] and then here at the community college level." Another faculty recalled that one of her college professors told the class to have higher aspirations than teaching at the secondary level. This comment had an impact. She said, "My original intent was to teach in the high school and that didn't pan out even though I've got those credentials. So when a position opened up at the community college, I received that position." Another participant stated that his interest in teaching was sparked when he was a graduate teaching assistant at a nearby university. He became an "academic gypsy," working as an adjunct faculty at three different institutions over two years. When a full-time position opened at his current community college, he took it and has been there since 1976.

The final two participants came to their faculty roles through other routes. A faculty of psychology was completing her Ph.D. at a local university and doing some consulting work. She commented, "I was teaching part time, and I was enjoying that more." She shifted her plans to seek a teaching position and was in the running for a position at a four-year college that did not pan out. When her current community college advertised for a full-time position, her outlook was different: "I was looking for full-time work, hopefully faculty. Essentially it was to stay in the area since I was dating at that time." She has been at the college since 2002. The final faculty participant has a Ph.D. in anatomy and physiology and a veterinary degree. She spent the first part of her career at research universities. In making her change to the community college, she reflected, "I decided I didn't want to write grants anymore, I was tired of publishing and perishing, and I have thirty-some-odd high-level publications. I just got tired of that competition for national grants and decided I just wanted to teach. So I looked around and thought a community college would be nice, and this was the only one that would consider me because I am so overqualified."

Despite the lack of planning that led each of the participants to their current faculty positions at the community college, a desire to teach was at the root of their decision making. Most were exposed to teaching during their college or graduate programs and began to seriously consider a community college option as they sought permanent employment. One faculty added, "It was much more rewarding to teach in a higher education community where I could see the difference that I could make in students' lives." The focus of community colleges on the teaching mission aligned with the value system of the faculty participants to be outstanding professors in their areas of specialty.

Connections to the Regional University. The proximity to a nearby university created strong links with the community college. Five of the six participants had obtained one or more degrees from the university, and several obtained their first taste of teaching as part of their graduate student responsibilities at the university. Indeed, some of the community college faculty also taught university classes in an adjunct capacity, closing the loop from university student to community college faculty to university adjunct.

It was often in graduate school that faculty had their first exposure to teaching. One faculty member noted, "When I first went to graduate school, it never occurred to me that I'd want to teach. I aspired to some big job where I'd be making six digits and traveling. Once I got into that, I hated it. I had started teaching as a grad assistant and I had always enjoyed that and thought it fit my personality better." The opportunity to teach during graduate programs offers a glimpse of what it means to teach at the collegiate level. It was often at graduate school that the decision was made not to pursue a doctorate and rather to go into teaching at a community college. Two of the participants held a Ph.D., and one had completed all work for the doctorate except the dissertation. For one, the decision not to pursue his Ph.D. coincided with a chance to be an adjunct at the community college. He added, "You get that sense of a calling when you do it, and you know this is what I'm supposed to be doing."

One faculty noted the importance of university connections: "I have friends at the [local university] and am in their reading groups, so I have people I can talk to. I still get to see my advisor at [state flagship university] and so I still have that intellectual stimulation." Working with graduate students at the university provided an additional venue for connections. The fact that several faculty also taught at the local university meant that information flowed between the two institutions and bridges were built. Students from the university often took classes at the community college to complement their university program or because of addition course options. Given the amount of transfer credit between the two institutions, faculty members were involved in articulation agreements and conversations regarding alignment of course sequencing. The community college recently opened a new campus branch that allowed it to expand its nursing and health profession programs. One of the faculty participants noted that the community college nursing program had the highest success rate for the certification exam in the state, making it sought after for university collaborations.

Practice.   The faculty participants noted different ways in which they stayed connected to practice. For some, this was an easier connection given the technical or vocational orientation of their programs. For those in the social sciences and humanities, the connections were with keeping current in the field and focusing on teaching and learning issues for their programs. One faculty member stated, "I evaluate the anatomy and physiology programs in the state at the community college level." She added, "I still get demands for my curriculum, and I do send outlines to other community colleges, especially nursing faculty, because they want to know why our nurses do so well."

The links to practice also occurred as community college students tried to apply their course work. One faculty recounted, "My students were motivated to learn in class; they could tell me stories of how they were taking the learning from the class back to work with them." She added that some students now contemplated psychology as a major as a result of her classes. An accounting faculty noted, "I try to surround myself with the experts that are practitioners to keep up to date, especially on the tax code." This faculty member worked to put programming online to help practitioners have increased access to course work and degree options.

Faculty participants were able to bring prior work experiences into their classroom teaching. Thus, the faculty member who spent years in the tourism business could bring in real examples to highlight the topics she was teaching. The faculty member who served as a business consultant could bring in scenarios from the field that provided examples for the student's textbook learning. Yet another faculty member works on professional presentations and writings to help other community college English teachers improve their practice.

Faculty members were also pulled to participate in more administrative job functions. Despite the ability to work on administrative projects, the faculty participants were adamant about their desire to remain in the classroom. One faculty member reflected, "I've been able to do what I like best, which is to teach. I've never really been interested in being strictly an administrator, but I can still do things that in a four-year school or even in a larger community college would have been reserved as administrative work." As faculty members in a community college, the other aspect of their practice was supporting the administrative infrastructure of the college.

Faculty Development Needs

Faculty development programs are in place at community colleges to help support faculty work. A national survey of community college vice presidents for academic affairs and faculty development center directors serves as the source of data regarding faculty development needs (Eddy, 2005, 2007). I selected 497 institutions from a master list obtained from the American Association of Community Colleges, and both the academic vice president and the faculty development director at each college received a survey. Response rates were 43 percent for vice presidents and 36 percent for those directing faculty development efforts. The overall response rate was 39 percent.

The portrait of faculty development at community colleges builds on the survey responses in which the majority of respondents worked in a rural location (46.8 percent), another 28.2 percent worked in a suburban college, 16.7 percent worked in urban locales, and another 8.3 percent worked in urban areas with suburban branch campuses. In general, this breakdown by location corresponds to the actual composition by location of all community colleges: 59.5 percent are rural, 21 percent are suburban, and 19.5 percent are urban.

In rating top program goals, survey participants indicated primary interest in creating a culture of teaching excellence, advancing new teaching and learning initiatives, and responding to individual faculty needs. Differences among rural and urban priorities were evident only when looking at secondary goals. Directors of programs in rural areas were more focused on programming that supported institutional and departmental needs, whereas urban leaders were not as focused on programming to support these types of faculty activities. As noted, because faculty generally come to the community college without planning for this career, support for learning more about teaching strategies is critical. Faculty working in rural areas often are pulled into administrative roles, making support for activities associated with college needs important. Faculty members in

Table 2.1.   Current Practices, New Directions, and Challenges

Current Practices—Important to Offer

1. Assessment of Student Learning Outcomes
2. Integrating Technology into Traditional Teaching
3. New Faculty Development

New Directions—Important to Offer

1. Program Assessment (e.g., Accreditation)
2. Training and Support for Part-Time/Adjunct Faculty
3. Unit/Program Evaluation

Challenges Facing Faculty

1. Assessment of Student Learning
2. Teaching Underprepared Students
3. Integrating Technology into Classroom Teaching

urban areas are able to be more focused on classroom responsibilities and require less programming in these areas.

To better understand the direction of faculty development programming, respondents were asked to rate current practices, new directions, and challenges on their campus. Currently, faculty developers are most focused on programs to help faculty learn how to assess student learning outcomes, integrate technology into their teaching, and help new faculty acclimate to their new roles. Notably, all of these areas are classroom-focused. Identification of important new directions included program assessment, training for part-time faculty, and program evaluation activities that focus on institutional needs versus individual needs (see Table 2.1). Finally, survey respondents identified the challenges facing faculty. The top challenges identified were assessment of student learning, teaching underprepared students, and integrating technology into classroom teaching. Taken together, this information indicates that faculty development programming is pulled in multiple directions, as are community college faculty.

Developing faculty members in community colleges requires a multifaceted approach. First, faculty must be prepared to meet their prime responsibility of classroom teaching. Preparation requires currency with new teaching strategies, incorporation of technology into classroom methods, and facing students who differ from those in the past with respect to demographics and preparation. Remedial work is increasingly pushed to the two-year college sector. Second, given the size of the full-time faculty base and the need to prepare for a changing of the guard of institutional leadership, faculty members increasingly take on leadership roles within the college. Assessment requirements, accreditation reporting, and strategic planning for curricular directions require faculty expertise in areas for which most are not prepared. Developing part-time faculty to their fullest capacity is also critical because upwards of 60 percent of faculty are part-timers (Cohen and Brawer, 2008). The survey indicates a gap between the demand for adjunct faculty training and current levels of training. Recruitment efforts and developing future faculty may become an area of heightened interest as retirements persist at community colleges.

Discussion and Conclusion

The changing nature of faculty work (Sorcinelli, Austin, Eddy, and Beach, 2006), coupled with demands to educate increasing numbers of Americans (Lumina Foundation, 2009), places pressure on community college faculty. The anticipated turnover in the ranks of community college faculty means that new faculty will be joining the ranks at two-year colleges. They will come to their positions with training in their profession, but not always training to teach (Sorcinelli, Austin, Eddy, and Beach, 2006). Changes are underway to rectify this lack of preparation. More universities are offering teaching certificates (among them are North Carolina State University, California State University-Dominguez Hills, University of Illinois, and Iowa State University), and more community colleges are providing training on classroom strategies.

Traditionally, recruitment of new faculty and succession planning has received scant attention in community colleges (Townsend and Twombly, 2007). The brewing of a perfect storm may change this perspective as senior faculty members retire, more students enroll in community colleges, and community colleges seek to offer baccalaureate degrees. This confluence of pressures on community college faculty requires a multifaceted response. New faculty are trying to fit in and figure out the institutional and teaching requirements for success, but they are not socialized for these roles in their university-based graduate programs. Following are suggestions for addressing the issues new faculty members face as outlined in this chapter.

Institutional Approaches.   New faculty members often come from nearby universities and start at the community college while they are graduate students to gain teaching experience and supplement their income. Community colleges need to capitalize on these connections and build bridges with university graduate programs. As new faculty are assimilated into the college, institutional leaders need to underscore the ties between institutional needs and individual faculty needs. Given the small size of full-time faculty bases, these individuals are pressed into institutional service on top of their current teaching obligations. It is critical to strategize how to leverage administrative work with faculty demands in the classroom. Rural community colleges may provide a template for these practices because faculty at these institutions are already juggling multiple responsibilities. Community college leaders should contemplate how to train a cadre of faculty leaders and prepare sitting midlevel leaders for upper-level positions. As institutions become flatter in operations, more collaborative leadership calls for increased roles for faculty members.

Faculty Development Planning.   There is a difference between the skills required for classroom teaching and being a content expert. New faculty needs support in figuring out their roles: how to work with diverse learners, use active learning and cooperative learning to help in classroom teaching, evaluate student learning, and be a good colleague. Faculty development directors can draw on the literature regarding faculty support programs such as mentoring new faculty, establishing professional learning communities, and making resources available online for easy access. It may help to share resources and programming with other regional community colleges or nearby universities. The availability of travel grants to allow faculty to attend teaching and learning workshops and network with other professionals can offer faculty an opportunity to bring new techniques back to campus. These trained faculty members can then lead development programs on campus to share their newly found expertise.

Individual Faculty Members.   Often interest in community college teaching is piqued through exposure to classroom teaching in graduate programs. As exemplified with the participants in this research, teaching is at the core of the faculty role at the community college. Faculty needs to take responsibility for becoming better at their trade. One means to do this is through professional development either at the college or in outside programs. For instance, the National Institute for Staff and Organizational Development (http://www.nisod.org/) hosts an annual conference focused on teaching and learning best practices. Ample books are available to help inform individual practice as well. It behooves new community college faculty to understand the culture of the community college setting, understand student learning needs, and become adept at using the technical tools to support classroom and online teaching.

New faculty members face multiple demands when they start on campus. Institutions and faculty development centers can help ease the transition with structured programs, and individual faculty can supplement this training with personal professional development. Because community college faculty members are not socialized to their new roles in four-year graduate programs, it is imperative that leaders help to fill this void and help shorten the learning curve for new faculty, which will increase the impact these new college members will have on the college.

References

Austin, A. E. "Preparing the Next Generation of Faculty: Graduate School as Socialization to the Academic Career." *Journal of Higher Education,* 2002, *73,* 94–122.

Cohen, A. M., and Brawer, F. B. *The American Community College.* (5th ed.) San Francisco: Jossey-Bass, 2008.

Eddy, P. L. "Faculty Development in Community Colleges: Surveying the Present, Preparing for the Future." *Journal of Faculty Development,* 2005, *20*(3), 143–152.

Eddy, P. L. "Faculty Development in Rural Community Colleges." In P. L. Eddy and J. Murray (eds.), *Rural Community Colleges: Teaching, Learning, and Leading in the Heartland.* New Directions for Community Colleges, no. 137. San Francisco: Jossey-Bass, 2007.

Eddy, P. L., and Gaston-Gales, J. "New Faculty on the Block: Issues of Stress and Support." *Journal of Human Behavior in the Social Environment,* 2008, *17*(1–2), 89–106.

Fugate, A. L., and Amey, M. J. "Career Stages of Community College Faculty: A Qualitative Analysis of Their Career Paths, Roles, and Development." *Community College Review,* 2000, *28*(1), 1–22.

Harris, S. G. "Organizational Culture and Individual Sensemaking: A Schema-Based Perspective." *Organization Science,* 1994, *5*(3), 309–321.

Holstein, J. A., and Gubrium, J. F. *The Active Interview.* Thousand Oaks, Calif.: Sage, 1995.

Lumina Foundation. *A Stronger Nation Through Higher Education: How and Why Americans Must Meet a "Big" Goal for College Attainment.* Indianapolis, Ind.: Lumina Foundation, 2009.

Murray, J. "Faculty Development in a National Sample of Community Colleges." *Community College Review,* 1999, *19*(6), 549–563.

Pratt, D. *Five Perspectives on Teaching in Adult and Higher Education.* Melbourne, Fla.: Krieger, 1998.

Ray, M. A. "The Richness of Phenomenology: Philosophic, Theoretic, and Methodological Concerns." In J. M. Morse (ed.), *Critical Issues in Qualitative Research Methods.* Thousand Oaks, Calif.: Sage, 1994.

Sorcinelli, M. D. "New Conceptions of Scholarship for a New Generation of Faculty Members." In G. H. Voegel (ed.), *Using Instructional Technology.* New Directions for Teaching and Learning, no. 9. San Francisco: Jossey-Bass, 2002.

Sorcinelli, M. D., Austin, A. E., Eddy, P. L., and Beach, A. L. *Creating the Future of Faculty Development: Learning from the Past, Understanding the Present.* San Francisco: Jossey-Bass/Anker Press, 2006.

Townsend, B. K., and Twombly, S. B. *Community College Faculty: Overlooked and Undervalued.* ASHE-ERIC Higher Education Report, 2007, no. 32-6. Hoboken, N.J.: Wiley, 2007.

Weick, K. E. *Sensemaking in Organizations.* Thousand Oaks, Calif.: Sage, 1995.

PAMELA L. EDDY *is associate professor in the department of Educational Policy, Planning, and Leadership at the College of William and Mary, Williamsburg, Virginia.*

This chapter examines Hillsborough Community College's approach to imparting to its faculty members an understanding of the community college as an educational institution.

An Approach to a Faculty Professional Development Seminar

Mary Bendickson, Karen Griffin

An effective faculty is essential to student success, and faculty development programs help sustain that effectiveness. Central to the faculty development programs at Hillsborough Community College (HCC) in Tampa, Florida, is the philosophy that they should lead to strengthened teaching and learning and, ultimately, improved student success. At the end of the 1990s, the college's administration and faculty agreed to include two graduate-level courses as a professional development requirement for nontenured faculty, based in part on the fact that many of the newly hired faculty had little or no experience with community colleges and college-level teaching expectations. These two courses, The Community College in Higher Education and Seminar in College Teaching, are offered by identical or similar names throughout the Florida university system, and the thought was that nontenured faculty would gain a well-grounded understanding of not only the Florida community college system but also the requirements of being a college faculty member.

Reactions to the required courses varied among the nontenured faculty. Those who had already earned doctorates, for example, felt that an alternative offered in-house at the college should be made available. Consequently, during fall 2007, a faculty committee was convened, which we chaired, to develop an in-house professional development seminar that was modeled after the graduate-level course, Community College in Higher Education. Plans for developing the in-house alternative to Seminar in College Teaching were to follow.

NEW DIRECTIONS FOR COMMUNITY COLLEGES, no. 152, Winter 2010 © 2010 Wiley Periodicals, Inc.
Published online in Wiley Online Library (wileyonlinelibrary.com) • DOI: 10.1002/cc.424

Developing the Seminar

The committee had several factors to consider in developing the seminar. At its first meeting in February 2008, the committee deliberated on whether the course should follow a traditional, blended, or fully online format. Course materials were discussed, along with requirements such as papers, presentations, or portfolios. The agenda for the meeting also included topics such as internships, Web site investigations, an overview of basic information and current issues to be covered in the seminar, guest speakers, field trips, who would teach the seminar, and the level of rigor as compared to a graduate-level course. By April 2008, the committee agreed to use Cohen and Brawer's *The American Community College* (2003) as the textbook, along with supplemental readings. The seminar would consist of forty-five contact hours (equivalent to a three-credit hour graduate course) with approximately fifteen hours devoted to in-class sessions, fifteen hours to online discussion board interactions, and fifteen hours to a group project and an individual project. Institutional syllabi from two public universities were reviewed to develop the concept further, as well as to refine course objectives. These particular syllabi were used for review because most of the HCC faculty who took the graduate-level courses did so at the two universities. One offered the course in a traditional format and the other in an online format. Both used Cohen and Brawer (2003) as a textbook for the course. Their syllabi provided the foundation for the seminar course objectives; the modular, hybrid (or blended) approach of the seminar; and the chapters that were to be covered each week. Rather than require additional readings beyond the Cohen and Brawer book, the committee recommended that additional readings would be a supplemental option, and a greater focus would be placed on learning more about HCC.

By the end of April, the concept was refined to include guest presenters for each in-class session, which, as the seminar leaders, we facilitated. The group project was developed to consist of a review of student services and its operations. This idea was agreed on based on the relative lack of familiarity that instructional faculty were believed to have with student services programs and functions. Because HCC is a multicampus institution with five locations, the participants were expected to visit at least two student services departments, attend at least one orientation for new students, and visit the college's Web site to determine how they would find information if they were new students. The outcome of this project would be a reflection paper from each student that would indicate what they learned from the experience as well as offer constructive recommendations.

This portion of the seminar created some discomfort among student services staff members when it was originally proposed. We explained that the intent was to educate, not to investigate deficiencies. This approach ameliorated the concerns and set the stage for positive interactions between the participants and student services staff. In fact, the experience was so positive that we were able to line up all five campuses for tours the subsequent summer, and participants were required to tour at least two of the five. Having all campuses involved became somewhat of a challenge to schedule but was successfully accomplished. In all cases, student services tours were scheduled on selected Friday mornings from 10:00 A.M. to 12:00 P.M., before the in-class session. For the 2008 group, only one tour for each campus was scheduled, and the entire group participated in touring both campuses. For the 2009 group, the student services deans provided several dates, and we worked with the participants to narrow them down to five tours.

The Seminar's First Year

By June, the syllabus was final, and eight participants had signed up. The seminar was offered in a hybrid mode, with sixteen hours delivered through classroom lecture and discussion, fifteen delivered electronically through participants' responses to questions we posted (participants were expected to respond to at least two questions each week), ten hours devoted to the group student services project, and five hours devoted to individual or smaller group projects. Participants were to write papers related to both the student services project and the individual or small group project, and they also had to write papers related to any in-class sessions that they missed. The seminar was offered on a pass/fail basis, and participants were expected to provide professional contributions in both the discussion board dialogues and their papers.

The in-class modules were organized using the Cohen and Brawer text (2003) as a guide. The speakers for each module had expertise related to the respective module. Module 1 covered Chapters One, Thirteen, and Fourteen and provided a historical overview and a discussion of current and future challenges. The presenters were the academic affairs dean and the director of the associate in arts program, both of whom had taken The Community College in Higher Education graduate course.

Module 2 covered Chapters Two and Seven and focused on students and student services. Guest presenters were student services representatives, including two student services deans and a student services staff member. Module 3 focused on faculty and instruction and Chapters Three and Six; a faculty member served as the presenter for that session. Module 4 addressed Chapters Four and Five, governance, finance, and administration; the presenters were the executive director of human resources, the vice president of academic affairs, and the chief financial officer.

Module 5 covered Chapter Eight on vocational education, and the presenters included the director of technical programs, a campus president, and the criminal justice program manager. The following week, module 6 focused on community and continuing education, and the presenters were the dean of business, who supervised apprenticeship programs, and the educator preparation institute officer, who coordinated the college's alternative educator certification program. Chapter Nine on developmental education came next, in module 7, and presenters were faculty members who taught developmental-level courses in math and English for nonnative speakers. The final module covered Chapter Eight on transfer education; the presenters were a campus president with a background in transfer advising and a grants officer whose dissertation focused on transfer issues that occur with students coming from a community college background and transferring to a university.

Following each in-class session, participants were required to respond to two questions posted on the online discussion board. The questions were designed to relate to the content covered in class and motivate the participants to seek sources beyond the textbook. Well-written and thoughtful responses were expected, and the majority of the participants met those expectations.

The discussion board questions were posted each week and related to the assigned readings. We specifically asked the participants to go beyond simply agreeing with the authors; in fact, the participants were encouraged to respond to each other and truly make it a discussion. For instance, the first module centered on the historical development of the community college, including key factors in its development. One of the questions posted that week was, "In the wake of today's trend toward grade inflation, explore various attitudes toward instruction and student performance from the dawn of the community college to the present." The participants responded heartily, speaking from their own student experiences and from their perspective as faculty, citing the Cohen and Brawer readings as requested.

Examples of other questions used in the discussion board included the following:

- Trace the effect of the "new students" on the growth of community colleges and how this has affected trends in higher education.
- Provide examples of the types of students you might encounter at a community college.
- Cohen and Brawer (2003) state, "If enrollment limitations mean that some students must be turned away, who shall they be? Those of lesser ability? Those with indistinct goals? Those who already have baccalaureate degrees?" If HCC had to limit its enrollment, what students should retain access?

It was not surprising that the last question drew the most discussion. The questions that elicited the most enthusiastic responses were ones that required an informed opinion about a controversial topic rather than ones that required simple demonstration of knowledge about a topic. For example, one question that generated a great deal of differing opinions asked participants to describe the pros and cons a faculty member would bring to the classroom if his or her teaching background was limited to high school instruction, a graduate school teaching assistant, university, or no teaching background but content mastery. If participants were able to choose only one among these four types, which would they recommend, and why? Most of the respondents provided reasons that they could not choose just one type and gave varying reasons that all or none could be an effective instructor. The question generated interaction between the respondents and became a topic of discussion at the in-class session.

For the individual project, the participants were encouraged to develop their own ideas that tied into the themes of the class. Three of the participants were on a college committee that sought to improve student success and retention. In a meeting of that committee, they realized that the goals of student success, retention, and the placement committee had parallels to the readings and discussion of the community college seminar. These three were able to work on a definition of student success that satisfied the individual project requirement of the seminar while also contributing significantly to the committee's goals in developing that definition. These faculty members ultimately presented their work to the president's cabinet, and the definition was adopted for the college.

Reflection papers on the student services experience (touring the sites, attending new student orientations, and reviewing the college's Web site) provided many positive observations and constructive recommendations. Two campuses were available for tours in 2008, and all five were available in 2009. Many of the participants commented on the value of touring the two campus sites. One was an old facility that had departments separated by a street. The student services dean commented on the problems of having to send students with disabilities from one department on one side of the street to another. Departments were cramped, the testing center was poorly designed, and the buildings in general were shabby. A new student services building was being planned, and the dean provided blueprints and described the advantages of the new facility, including having a more streamlined approach to admitting and enrolling students of all types. The concept of a generalist desk to triage students came in part from the second campus the students toured. This campus had a virtually new student services building with an initial point of entry that allowed staff who were student services generalists to quickly direct students to the appropriate departments. The facility was spacious, with plenty of light and appealing furniture that lent a student-friendly appearance.

Many of the reflection papers commented on the information overload that occurred in new student orientations. One faculty member, for example, commented that he already knew or had at least been exposed to much of the information, yet was struggling to take it all in during the orientation and wondered how new students would cope. Each campus provides orientations in different formats. The largest campus provides three different types of orientation depending on whether the students are not native English speakers, whether they are students needing remediation, or whether they are college-ready, but other campuses are limited to providing orientations in large rooms with large groups of students.

Finally, many of the participants commented on the college Web site, which at the time was not easy to navigate. One participant chose the opportunity to develop a critique and recommendations for improvement to the site as his individual project.

The format of the seminar was modified as it was implemented. We were open with the faculty participants and welcomed their suggestions and feedback. There were numerous positive comments and several suggestions. More than one stated that they appreciated the opportunity to learn more about HCC and were going to spread the word to others to encourage them to take the seminar the next time it was offered.

One of the comments focused on the desire of the participants to have more class time to continue the discussion from the week's discussion board. They felt that the speakers who were invited to present on a particular topic made it impossible to have the discussion that they wanted. The suggestion was specifically aimed at not taking time away from the speakers, but restructuring the time to allow group conversation. As a result of this suggestion, the second year's schedule allotted time for continued conversation about the week's discussion board postings. In addition, the 2009 group was required to respond to the question that was posted during the week prior to the in-class session in which the topic would be discussed. With the 2008 group, the participants responded after the in-class session and had several questions from which to choose, some based on simply displaying knowledge of the topic and others requiring informed opinions. We believed that by limiting the 2009 group to one question that represented a combination of display of knowledge and informed opinion, the group would have a better opportunity to interact and discuss their thoughts at the upcoming in-class session. However, with a different group of faculty members in the second year, it quickly became apparent that this group did not feel the need for more discussion. When each session was opened with leading questions taken from their discussion board postings, the response was minimal, and continued conversation died off quickly. In fact, on more than one occasion, we had to remind the participants that the responses were supposed to be written in an informed, scholarly manner with facts to support opinions. One participant was consistently on target, but some of the others clearly dashed off responses. We will give consideration to changing the format next summer based on this year's experience.

The Second Year

In presenting the seminar the second year, we incorporated suggestions from the prior year's group. Dealing with a different group of individual faculty members, however, brought out unexpected results. Members of the first year's group had had no problem in selecting a suitable topic for the projects. The distinction between the group project on student services and the individual project on a topic of their choosing was clear. The first participants all submitted work that was in keeping with our intent.

Because the first year's projects had gone so smoothly, it was a surprise that the second year's projects were much more problematic. This group struggled to understand the projects and find suitable topics for their individual project. When the individual projects were presented, at least half the topics chosen were not in keeping with the thrust of the seminar. Part of the struggle may have been caused by circumstances that prevented both of us from being present at all of the in-class sessions. Consequently, our communication with each other was impaired and at times we inadvertently presented conflicting information to the students. However, we remained puzzled by the struggle because we had deliberately built in time for a thorough orientation at the beginning of the session to review the syllabus and answer questions. In some cases, participants simply did not pay sufficient attention during the orientation or review their syllabus after that. One outcome from this experience is that we will reword portions of the syllabus to refer to a "student services project" rather than a "group project" and to use "individual project" rather than "individual or small group project." If, with the individual project, two or more participants wish to collaborate, they will need to take the initiative to ask the instructors. Another outcome is that the instructors will provide examples of individual projects that would be considered appropriate.

Ultimately, based on the performance of some of the participants, we were left with a decision of whether to award a satisfactory completion to the individuals who participated only minimally and had submitted less-than-adequate individual projects. We decided to award satisfactory completions but also to be clearer to future participants in describing expectations for the student services project as well as the individual project.

One notable project presented this year centered on new faculty orientation. A computer science faculty member chose to use his computer skills to develop a plan that could be used at subsequent new faculty orientations to provide information for the new members for review after the orientation. The quantity of information that new faculty are given can be overwhelming because there is a steep learning curve in coming to a new institution and getting classes ready to go on the first day. This project was very much on target with the seminar expectations and may also be put into action in future new faculty orientations.

The Future

Of the summer 2009 and 2010 participants who have responded to our request for feedback on the Community College Seminar, several comments have been positive. We will seek input from additional sources, such as the academic deans and the student services deans, in planning the summer 2011 session. They will likely retain the project of having participants tour student services sites and functions, because this continues to be a revealing experience for instructional faculty. Learning more about the student services side of the college helps to improve communication between academics and student services and can help to improve students' experiences at the college.

In addition to the Community College Seminar, the Seminar on College Teaching was offered this summer, and a faculty member facilitated and included guest presenters. Feedback was positive, and that seminar will be offered again next summer as well. Both seminars provide a valuable resource for faculty development, and both will remain flexible enough in format to meet faculty development needs.

Reference

Cohen, A. M., and Brawer, F. B. *The American Community College.* (4th ed.) San Francisco: Jossey-Bass, 2003.

MARY BENDICKSON *is dean of associate of arts, humanities and communications at the Dale Mabry Campus of Hillsborough Community College in Tampa, Florida.*

KAREN GRIFFIN *is the director of associate of arts for Hillsborough Community College in Tampa, Florida.*

This chapter reviews the literature regarding the issues and challenges facing rural community colleges in their efforts to attract qualified candidates for full-time faculty vacancies. It discusses factors related to the socialization of faculty into the rural community college environment and provides recommendations for policy and practice.

Faculty Issues in Rural Community Colleges

Brent D. Cejda

The 2005 Carnegie classifications of colleges offering the associate degree identified 1,043 publicly controlled two-year colleges. Among these institutions, 594 (57 percent) are identified as rural serving. Categorizing community colleges as rural, suburban, or urban serving was based on Primary Metropolitan Statistical Areas (PMSAs), Metropolitan Statistical Areas (MSAs), and population. Associate degree colleges designated as rural serving are located within PMSAs or MSAs with a population of fewer than 500,000 people (using the 2000 Census) or are not located within a PMSA or MSA.

An important consideration in examining faculty issues facing rural community colleges is the number of full-time faculty employed by these institutions and the number of students they serve. As indicated above, 57 percent of public community colleges are designated as rural. Using the measure of annual unduplicated head count enrollment, rural institutions served 36 percent of all community college enrollments in academic year 2003 (Hardy, 2005). Maldanado (2006) found that 42 percent of the full-time faculty employed by geographically designated community colleges held appointments at rural-serving institutions. The number of rural community colleges, the percentage of the community college population they serve, and the proportion of full-time faculty they employ point to the importance of examining issues related to recruiting the next generation of faculty for this institutional type.

NEW DIRECTIONS FOR COMMUNITY COLLEGES, no. 152, Winter 2010 © 2010 Wiley Periodicals, Inc.
Published online in Wiley Online Library (wileyonlinelibrary.com) • DOI: 10.1002/cc.425

The Rural Environment

The majority of the literature on the community college faculty labor market has focused on the community college as a whole (Gahn and Twombly, 2001, for example). The fields of science, technology, engineering, and math (STEM) are expected to be a primary area of competition for faculty as the community college assumes greater responsibility for workforce preparation (Patton, 2006). In addition, Burnett (2004) reported that community colleges were experiencing faculty shortages in special education and English as a Second Language. Using data from a 2007 survey, Rankin (2009) found that 48 percent of the chief academic officers (CAOs) at rural community colleges indicated that it is difficult to recruit qualified full-time faculty to the community college, in comparison to 45 percent of the responding suburban CAOs and 17 percent of the responding urban CAOs. Pennington, Williams, and Karvonen (2006) found that the most consistent challenge identified by ten rural community college presidents was the inability to find qualified employees for all positions, including the faculty. Neither of these resources, however, presented specific information on why rural institutions face this challenge.

Murray (2007) points out that there are fewer local residents qualified for faculty positions in rural communities. Therefore, most faculty who are hired must move their residence. Vander-Staay (2005) suggested a number of reasons that individuals might prefer a faculty position at a rural community college, including the lifestyle and shorter commutes to work. Other authors, however, have stressed that the lack of cultural, social, shopping, and recreational amenities in rural areas creates a disadvantage in recruiting new faculty (Leist, 2005; Murray, 2005; Wolfe and Strange, 2003). The environment of the college is another consideration in recruiting faculty to rural community colleges.

Providing a comprehensive educational program to a relatively small population of students has created economy-of-scale issues for rural community colleges (Pennington, Williams, and Karvonen, 2006). Faculty are often the only individual teaching in their respective fields and thus have sole responsibility for the curriculum (Vander-Staay, 2005; Murray, 2007). When asked to describe a faculty position, a rural community college president explained, "Our physics instructors also will teach astronomy and maybe geology . . . they [the full-time faculty] are the ones who are responsible for writing the curriculum and the requirements" (Twombly, 2005, p. 434). Murray and Cunningham (2004) found that new faculty members at rural community colleges identified the number of classes included in their workload as a frustration or a disappointment. In addition to the course requirements, rural community college faculty are often expected to perform noninstructional duties (Glover, Simpson, and Waller, 2009) or assume instructional-related responsibilities in tutoring centers or managing science and technology labs without the support of a lab director (Eddy, 2007).

NEW DIRECTIONS FOR COMMUNITY COLLEGES • DOI: 10.1002/cc

The value that community colleges place on teaching is well documented (Flannigan, Jones, and Moore, 2004; Gahn and Twombly, 2001; Sprouse, Ebbers, and King, 2008; Twombly, 2005). The challenge of providing instruction that meets the needs of all learners is heightened at the community college as a result of open door admissions policies that result in a wide variety of students with different levels of college preparation in the same classes (Sprouse, Ebbers, and King, 2008; Twombly, 2005). Sax, Astin, Korn, and Gilmartin (1999) found that 80 percent of community college faculty members perceived that their students were not prepared for college-level work. In terms of rural community college faculty, Murray and Cunningham's (2004) analysis indicated the overwhelming perception that students were not prepared for college-level work. In addition, they reported faculty dismay regarding the lack of motivation displayed by students attending rural community colleges.

Fit with the Rural Environment

The unique aspects of living and working in a rural environment illustrate the importance of the fit of the faculty member with the college and the community. In an examination of the hiring practices at three community colleges (Twombly, 2005), fit was identified as a more important consideration at the rural community college in comparison to the suburban and urban community colleges included in the study. Leist (2007) references the importance of fit in relation to presidential vacancies at rural community colleges. Interviews with rural community college leaders (Pennington, Williams, and Karvonen, 2006) indicated that all employees, including faculty, either fit into the college or did not.

Financial Challenges

The economic climate in rural America has consequences for community colleges seeking to hire the next generation of faculty. One illustration of the climate is found in statistics presented by Mosley and Miller (2004), who found that among the nearly four hundred counties in the United States that have experienced poverty rates of 20 percent or more in each decade from the 1960s through the 1990s, 95 percent are rural. Several authors contend that funding inequities between rural and nonrural community colleges continue (Hardy and Katsinas, 2007; Pennington, Williams, and Karvonen; 2006; Waller and others, 2007).

Murray (2007) emphasized that the income levels in rural areas meant that community colleges were not as able to charge higher tuition to offset declines in local, state, and federal aid. As a result, rural community colleges may not have sufficient funding for high-cost curricula, increased faculty salaries, or professional development programs. Hardy and Katsinas (2007) suggested that financial considerations also affected important services; they found that 47 percent of rural community colleges provided on-campus child care in comparison to 67 percent of suburban and 75 percent of urban community colleges.

For this chapter, the most pressing financial issue facing rural community colleges is the salaries they are able to provide faculty. Glover, Simpson, and Waller (2009) examined salary differences using the Texas Higher Education Coordinating Board's designation of the respective fifty public community college districts in the state as metropolitan or nonmetropolitan. Their study included data for 2000 and 2005. In 2000, the average faculty salary among the nineteen nonmetropolitan districts was $5,480 less than the average faculty salary among the thirty-one metropolitan districts. For 2005 the salary difference increased to $6,612. Further analyses indicated that the salary differential for both years was statistically significant.

Maldanado (2006) compared national 2003 salary data among the geographic community college designations. He reported average salaries of $46,535 at rural-serving institutions, $59,960 at suburban-serving institutions, and $55,942 at urban-serving institutions. Maldanado's study also revealed salary differences between the enrollment subcategories of rural-serving community colleges: $41,382 at small colleges (fewer than 2,500 unduplicated head count), $44,193 at medium colleges (unduplicated head count of 2,501 to 7,500), and $51,514 at large colleges (unduplicated head count greater than 7,500). In addition, Maldanado found that the average salary of faculty at rural-serving community colleges with collective bargaining was $9,744 higher than at rural-serving institutions without collective bargaining.

The data indicate that when salary is considered, rural community colleges are not competitive with suburban and urban institutions. Therefore, information such as cost of living and quality of life must be developed in times of competitive hiring if faculty searches at rural community colleges are to be successful. Given the salary differences among rural institutions by size and collective bargaining status, specific place-based aspects related to each respective community and service area become important rather than the more generic rural-versus-urban arguments.

The Hiring Process

In presenting the need for her study, Twombly (2005) argued that little is known about community college faculty hiring processes. Flannigan, Jones, and Moore (2004) found a homogeneous selection process in the hiring of faculty. They described this process as one that uses standardized job descriptions, is limited in the advertising of positions, and places an emphasis on credentials and experience as qualifying factors for the candidates. Twombly (2005) examined the hiring of full-time arts and sciences faculty in three community colleges: one rural, one in a suburban county, and one urban. She found that although the rural community college advertised internally, regionally, and nationally, hiring was regional in nature. She also was surprised to find that only one of the three institutions specified community college teaching experience as a preferred qualification.

A primary reason for the paucity of research on recruitment and hiring appears to be that not many individuals have indicated that they aspired to a career as a community college faculty member. Fugate and Amey (2000) summarized that community college faculty as a whole have not consciously pursued a community college teaching career. In their study of rural community college faculty, Murray and Cunningham (2004) found that only three of forty-five participants had purposefully pursued a faculty appointment in community colleges. Interviews with ten recently hired community college faculty led Twombly (2005) to conclude that these were individuals who preferred an emphasis on teaching over research and accepted positions at the community college because of that emphasis. Interviews with forty-five faculty members in rural community colleges (Murray and Cunningham, 2004) revealed that the faculty members who were most satisfied with teaching at a rural community college were those comfortable with living and working in a rural community, enjoyed the challenge of teaching students with varying levels of college readiness, and found intrinsic value in their students' accomplishments.

Socialization

Sprouse, Ebber, and King (2008) pointed to the financial investment in faculty in calling for the creation of quality faculty development programs. A similar argument can be made for creating viable faculty recruitment and hiring strategies. Although limited, previous findings point to the value that can be gained by consulting with existing faculty about their satisfactions and dissatisfactions. Moreover, the relationship between socialization and retention emphasizes the need to begin socialization into the rural community college with the search, not after hiring.

Studies of academic careers have indicated that individuals who have a clear understanding of the expectations of the position are more successfully socialized into the profession (Gaff and Lambert, 1996) and socialization has been identified as an important factor in the decision of a new employee to remain with the employing institution and the career (Aryee, Chay, and Chew, 1994). As Murray (2007) summarized, "Individuals whose expectations of the job are more closely aligned with the reality of the job are more likely to experience job satisfaction, and therefore, more likely to find a career fit" (p. 60). The fact that the fit between the person and the environment has been identified as the primary factor in job satisfaction (Bertz and Judge, 1994) and the findings on fit in a rural environment

(Leist, 2007; Pennington, Williams, and Karvonen, 2006; Twombly, 2005) support the contention that rural community colleges should initiate socialization at the beginning of a search.

Suggestions to Improve Practice

Premack and Wanous (1985) emphasize the importance of realistic job previews in recruiting and retaining employees. Murray and Cunningham (2004) suggest that if rural community colleges introduced prospective faculty to the realities of the rural community college, both recruitment and retention efforts would improve. In suggesting improvements in vacancy announcements for rural community college presidents, Leist (2007) emphasized the need to clearly explain the rurality of the institution, including the geography of the area, the size of the college's service area, economic and educational composition, and cultural information. These suggestions also make sense in terms of advertisements for faculty positions.

Realistic information about position responsibilities is equally important. Based on previous studies (Murray and Cunningham, 2004; Twombly, 2005), announcements should clearly indicate the specific classes that an individual would be expected to teach, responsibilities regarding the curriculum, any instructional support (such as lab supervision or tutoring), and other expectations. Of fundamental importance is the common practice that rural community college faculty are required to teach a number of courses in a variety of related disciplines. One view of a faculty career is from the disciplinary perspective. Rural community college faculty who are satisfied with their positions view the faculty career from a teaching perspective, and this viewpoint should be stressed where applicable. Information on the student population of the institution as a whole and the typical students the individual would experience in the classes they would teach are also important to creating a realistic preview.

Given the anticipated numbers of vacancies, rural community colleges will need to become proactive in recruiting the next generation of faculty. The current practice of self-selection, where individuals who like the rural environment and fit into the college stay and those who do not leave, could prove financially costly and will endanger these institutions from meeting their mission as learner-centered institutions. Improving the search and hiring process by creating realistic job previews, thus initiating socialization earlier in the process, will improve recruitment and retention, but other strategies will be required as well.

Murray and Cunnigham (2004) found that a number of rural community college faculty mentioned a faculty contact at the institution as someone who informed them of the vacancy or encouraged them to apply for the position. Rural community college leaders might solicit names from existing faculty as a strategy to create a pool of potential faculty. Additional strategies suggested for rural community colleges include recruiting dual-career couples, creating a teaching fellows program, or tracking former students who may desire to return to the community college they attended (Murray, 2007). Two of these strategies point to the importance of collaborative efforts between the community college and other educational organizations. Developing joint advertisements with K-12 schools or four-year universities in the service area could increase the pool of candidates. It is unlikely that one rural community college could develop a teaching fellows program with a four-year institution, but such a program for all community colleges in a state would, at a minimum, expose a greater number of graduate students to the possibilities of teaching in a rural environment.

Rural community colleges employ 42 percent of the full-time community college faculty. Therefore, it is important to consider the unique challenges and issues they face in anticipation of a significant turnover of faculty. Improvements in current recruitment and hiring processes among rural institutions will also be beneficial to suburban and urban community colleges as they consider the successful approaches that their rural colleagues implement.

References

Aryee, S., Chay, Y. W., and Chew, J. "An Investigation of the Predictors and Outcomes of Career Commitment in Three Career Stages." *Journal of Vocational Behavior,* 1994, *44,* 1–16.

Bertz, J.R.D., and Judge, T. A. "Person-Organization Fit and the Theory of Work Adjustment: Implications for Satisfaction, Tenure, and Career Success." *Journal of Vocational Behavior,* 1994, *44,* 32–52.

Burnett, S. "Using Our Imagination." *Community College Week,* September 27, 2004, pp. 6–8.

Eddy, P. L. "Faculty Development in Rural Community Colleges." In P. L. Eddy and J. Murray (eds.), *Rural Community Colleges: Teaching, Learning, and Leading in the Heartland.* New Directions for Community Colleges, no. 137. San Francisco: Jossey-Bass, 2007.

Flannigan, S. J., Jones, B. R., and Moore Jr., W. "An Exploration of Faculty Hiring Practices in Community Colleges." *Community College Journal of Research and Practice,* 2004, *28,* 823–836.

Fugate, A. L., and Amey, M. J. "Career Stages of Community College Faculty: A Qualitative Analysis of Their Career Paths, Roles and Development." *Community College Review,* 2000, *28,* 1–22.

Gaff, J. G., and Lambert, L. M. "Socializing Future Faculty to the Values of Undergraduate Education." *Change,* 1996, *4,* 39–45.

Gahn, S., and Twombly, S. B. "Dimensions of the Community College Faculty Labor Market." *Review of Higher Education,* 2001, *24,* 259–282.

Glover, L. C., Simpson, L. A., and Waller, L. R. "Disparities in Salaries: Metropolitan Versus Nonmetropolitan Community College Faculty." *Community College Journal of Research and Practice,* 2009, *33,* 47–54.

Hardy, D. E. "A Two-Year College Typology for the 21st Century: Updating and Utilizing the Katsinas-Lacy Classification System." *Dissertation Abstracts International,* 2005, *66*(7), 2508A. (UMNI No. AAT 3181046).

Hardy, D. E., and Katsinas, S. G. "Classifying Community Colleges: How Rural Community Colleges Fit." In P. L. Eddy and J. Murray (eds.), *Rural Community Colleges:*

Teaching, Learning, and Leading in the Heartland. New Directions for Community Colleges, no. 137. San Francisco: Jossey-Bass, 2007.

Leist, J. E. "Exemplary Rural Community College Presidents: A Case Study of How Well Their Professional Qualities Mirror Job Advertisements." Unpublished doctoral dissertation, Texas Tech University, 2005.

Leist, J. E. "'Ruralizing' Presidential Job Advertisements." In P. L. Eddy and J. Murray (eds.), *Rural Community Colleges: Teaching, Learning, and Leading in the Heartland.* New Directions for Community Colleges, no. 137. San Francisco: Jossey-Bass, 2007.

Maldanado, J. F. "A National Analysis of Faculty Salary and Benefits in Public Community Colleges, Academic Year 2003–2004." Unpublished doctoral dissertation, University of North Texas, 2006.

Mosley, J. M., and Miller, K. K. *What the Research Says About Spatial Variations in Factors Affecting Poverty.* Corvallis: Oregon State University, Rural Poverty Research Center, 2004.

Murray, J. P. "Meeting the Needs of New Faculty at Rural Community Colleges." *Community College Journal of Research and Practice,* 2005, *29,* 215–232.

Murray, J. P. "Recruiting and Retaining Rural Community College Faculty." In P. L. Eddy and J. Murray (eds.), *Rural Community Colleges: Teaching, Learning, and Leading in the Heartland.* New Directions for Community Colleges, no. 137. San Francisco: Jossey-Bass, 2007.

Murray, J. P., and Cunningham, S. "New Rural Community College Faculty Members and Job Satisfaction." *Community College Review,* 2004, *32,* 19–38.

Patton, M. *Teaching by Choice: Cultivating Exemplary Community College STEM Faculty.* Washington, D.C.: Community College Press, 2006.

Pennington, K., Williams, M., and Karvonen, M. "Challenges Facing Rural Community Colleges: Issues and Problems Today and over the Past Thirty Years." *Community College Journal of Research and Practice,* 2006, *30,* 641–655.

Premack, S. L., and Wanous, J. P. "A Meta-Analysis of Realistic Job Preview Experiments." *Journal of Applied Psychology,* 1985, *70,* 706–719.

Rankin, K. R. *Perceptions of Institutional Chief Executive Officers and Chief Academic Officers of Community Colleges Regarding Issues, Problems, and Challenges.* Unpublished doctoral dissertation, University of Alabama, 2009.

Sax, L. J., Astin, A. W., Korn, W. S., and Gilmartin, S. K. *The American College Teacher: National Norms for the 1998–1999 HERI Faculty Survey.* Los Angeles: University of California, Higher Education Research Institute, 1999.

Sprouse, M., Ebbers, L. H., and King, A. R. "Hiring and Developing Quality Community College Faculty." *Community College Journal of Research and Practice,* 2008, *32,* 985–998.

Twombly, S. B. "Values, Policies, and Practices Affecting the Hiring Process for Full-Time Arts and Sciences Faculty in Community Colleges." *Journal of Higher Education,* 2005, *76,* 423–447.

Vander-Staay, S. L. "In the Right Direction." *Chronicle of Higher Education,* June 10, 2005, p. B5.

Waller, L., and others. "Texas Community College Funding: Non-Metropolitan and Metropolitan Ad Valorem Tax Rates and Revenue." *Community College Journal of Research and Practice,* 2007, *33,* 563-573.

Wolfe, J. R., and Strange, C. C. "Academic Life at the Franchise: Faculty Culture in a Rural Two-Year Branch Campus." *Review of Higher Education,* 2003, *26*(3), 345–362.

BRENT D. CEJDA *is associate professor in the Department of Educational Administration at the University of Nebraska-Lincoln and executive director of the National Council of Instructional Administrators.*

This chapter explores the attractiveness of community colleges for female faculty. It highlights several areas that need continued improvement to attract and retain female faculty and provides recommendations for changes to policies and practices.

Hiring and Recruiting Female Faculty

Jaime Lester, Trudy Bers

The picture of gender equity in the faculty ranks at community colleges is murky. Community colleges are generally more inclusive to female faculty as compared to four-year institutions. Women represent 49 percent of full-time and 50 percent of part-time community college faculty, a stark contrast to the low numbers of female faculty in four-year institutions (Cataldi, Fahimi, and Bradburn, 2005). Female faculty at community colleges also receive similar rates of compensation. West and Curtis (2006) found that women's faculty salaries are 81 percent as a percentage of men's in all public institutions and 95 percent at public two-year colleges. In contrast, gender segregation continues in traditionally feminized disciplines—professional and academic disciplines that are historically populated by women. English, education, human science, health professions, and library science are primarily dominated by women, with over 65 percent of the faculty being female, while more than 70 percent of the faculty in physical science and security and protective services are male faculty (National Center for Education Statistics, 2009).

This chapter explores the attractiveness of community colleges for female faculty in order to understand why female faculty enter community colleges overall but in traditionally feminized disciplines. We also highlight the areas that need continued improvement and provide recommendations for how current leaders and faculty can continue to attract women to the community college and diversify the academic and vocational disciplines in which they are underrepresented.

New Directions for Community Colleges, no. 152, Winter 2010 © 2010 Wiley Periodicals, Inc.
Published online in Wiley Online Library (wileyonlinelibrary.com) • DOI: 10.1002/cc.426

One key reason for focusing on female faculty is the overall importance of community colleges writ large. They play a substantial but little-recognized role in providing postsecondary education, particularly for low-income and minority students. President Obama's American Graduation Initiative has recognized community colleges as critical resources for training and retraining the workforce (Obama, 2009). A second key reason for focusing on female faculty is the value they provide in mentoring and serving as role models for students. For example, Starobin and Laanan (2008) found that female faculty in science, mathematics, engineering, and technology (STEM) fields promote retention and transfer among female students. A third reason is the anticipated shortage of community college teachers and the need for institutions to focus on hiring quality instructors and invest in their professional development (Strouse, Ebbers, and King, 2008). Hiring processes affect recruitment and selection, and if these areas are left unexamined, institutions may inadvertently find themselves perpetuating their existing employee patterns rather than taking advantage of the opportunity to reshape the faculty. But given the number of female faculty currently employed in this sector, one may argue that women will continue to flock to community colleges and that leaders and senior faculty do not need to consider new ways to attract women to the faculty ranks and retain them.

The Attractiveness of Community Colleges to Female Faculty

One of the main reasons documented in the research literature for women choosing the community college is the desire to achieve balance between their personal and professional lives (Sallee, 2008; Townsend and LaPaglia, 2000; Wolf-Wendel, Ward, and Twombly, 2007). Many studies confirm that female faculty in four-year institutions delay or forgo childbearing because they see family as incompatible with academe and the requirements for tenure and promotion (Armenti, 2004; Drago and others, 2005; Mason and Goulden, 2002; Ward and Wolf-Wendel, 2004). Female faculty note that they chose the community college because they are able to teach while raising a family (Wolf-Wendel, Ward, and Twombly, 2007). Shorter time to tenure, an emphasis on teaching in tenure decisions, and more variable faculty roles such as part-time faculty work are noted reasons that women perceive community colleges as more family friendly than four-year colleges and universities (Grumet, 1988).

Community colleges are also attractive to women because of their historical connection to female-dominated professions and their commitment to social justice. For example, the American Association of Community Colleges (2004) notes that two-year institutions have been historically accessible to women due to the initial focus on preparing grammar school teachers. The National League for Nursing (2009) found that in 2006-2007, approximately 60 percent of students admitted to and graduating from prelicensure nursing programs were in associate degree curricula, which are offered primarily at community colleges. Still another feature of community colleges that makes them attractive to female faculty is the opportunity afforded to those who want to be college presidents. In 2006, 28.8 percent of associate degree institutions had women presidents versus 13.8 percent of doctoral, 21.5 percent of master's, and 23.2 percent of baccalaureate institutions (American Council on Education, 2007). Finally, salary inequities are generally nonexistent in community colleges, a stark contrast from the entrenched salary disparities in four-year institutions. A lack of salary disparities has been attributed to the presence of unions that negotiate standard contracts, with both starting and subsequent salaries determined by degrees, years of experience, and participation in a variety of professional activities. Rarely are there provisions for salary differentials based on discipline or merit awards for publication or grant acquisition.

Areas for Improvement

The positive perceptions and high level of job satisfaction by female community college faculty do not tell the whole story. Female faculty generally feel as if the community college is an equitable environment, particularly in contrast to other sectors of higher education. Huber (1998) found that 85 percent of women report being treated fairly at the community colleges. A more recent study by Hagedorn and Laden (2002) also report an overwhelmingly positive perception of community colleges by female faculty. Women generally do not view community colleges as discriminatory and feel as if they are treated equally. Yet in-depth qualitative studies suggest more complicated experiences and perceptions of women community college faculty and point to some areas that require improvement. For example, female faculty are more likely than their male counterparts to perceive gender discrimination (Hagedorn and Laden, 2002; Townsend and LaPaglia, 2000). Also, one study found that female faculty at a rural campus experienced a negative climate (Wolfe and Strange, 2003). Female faculty are also susceptible to workplace bullying (Lester, 2009), experience conflicts between personal and professional lives (Sallee, 2008), and are expected to perform in stereotypical feminine ways, such as playing a maternal role with students and colleagues (Lester, 2008). In this section, we suggest three areas that illustrate the ways that community colleges can work to improve policies, practices, and cultures to become even more attractive to female faculty in the future.

Feminization of Disciplines and Academic Departments.   Kanter (1977) suggested that when women are a numerical minority in organizations, they are given a tokenized status; they serve as representatives of a group, not as individuals. In certain departments in community colleges that are historically dominated by one gender group, either men or women, the minority group takes on the token status. Lester (2008) observed that female faculty in male-dominated departments were expected to perform traditional "women's work" and serve as representatives of the women's perspective. A female welding instructor, for example, was also asked to perform in stereotypical feminine ways (taking notes in meetings and listening to the personal problems of colleagues and students) as a member of the department and among her male students. Community colleges can improve the overall culture of the institution and be more gender equitable by disaggregating the demographic data to look within individual departments. Aggregate numbers are important and show gender inclusiveness of community colleges, but most of the interactions and work of teaching are done within the context of departments. Once the data are disaggregated, departments need to evaluate their own practices to assess whether women are underrepresented or marginalized. Inappropriate behaviors may be explicit (always asking females to take notes at meetings, for example) or more subtle (for example, assigning women to introductory courses and reserving higher-level courses for males in the department).

Lack of Work-Life Policies.   While community colleges are reputed to be more comfortable environments than four-year institutions for faculty trying to balance work and life responsibilities, issues do exist. Sallee (2008) found that faculty in community colleges report at least one major life event in the previous three years that affected their professional lives, and that more than two-thirds of the faculty report that they often choose between their personal and professional lives. In addition, Sallee (2008) found that faculty are not aware of any policies that assist with creating a balance or mediating the impact of life events.

While other sectors of higher education are establishing policies for paid leave after childbirth, paid dependent care, modified duties, reduced appointments, and a break in the tenure clock, community colleges do not generally have such policies. Faculty often rely on the goodwill of colleagues, saved sick time, and unpaid leave to manage personal conflicts (Sallee, 2008). This is not to suggest that four-year institutions are very progressive in the area of work-life balance; in fact, only a handful have policies beyond the option for faculty to delay their tenure clock for one year for a major life event. Therefore, if community colleges want to maintain their attractiveness for women or actively recruit female faculty (or both), they need to consider new work-life polices and campaigns to make these policies visible. Moreover, policies are not singularly effective. Campuses need to create a culture of work-life balance by ensuring that faculty know what benefits are available to them and that using these benefits is acceptable and encouraged.

Interpersonal Gender Dynamics.   An often overlooked area that has implications for faculty participation in governance, job satisfaction, and retention is interpersonal gender dynamics that shape the departmental culture. In an ethnographic study of female community college faculty, Lester (2008, 2009) found that female faculty often experience workplace bullying, perceive they are victimized by other faculty colleagues, and feel pressured to perform stereotypical gender roles such as taking notes in a secretarial role in a department meeting. As a result of these gender dynamics, female faculty often isolate themselves from interaction with other faculty in governance and department meetings. They also tailor their gender behavior to those expectations regardless of their own gender identity. These issues have particular significance to faculty governance, where interpersonal interactions are heightened by committee work and the political nature of the leadership roles. In a study of faculty governance and gender at California community colleges, Lester and Lucas (2008) found that women did not perceive discrimination overall, but did feel excluded from powerful committees such as those that oversaw budgets.

Recommendations for Hiring and Retention

In order to address the areas that need improvement and attract and retain female faculty, we describe several specific recommendations to improve the feminization of academic disciplines, work-life balance, and interpersonal gender dynamics.

First, community colleges can recruit faculty into traditionally male-dominated positions and improve interpersonal gender dynamics by addressing biases within both hiring committees and the faculty at large. For example, department chairs and faculty on search committees may be asked to participate in professional development training to uncover and address subtle biases that serve as barriers to hiring women. Some institutions ask search committee members to take an implicit bias test. Individuals are given pictures of men and women in nontraditional gender roles and are asked to respond to a series of questions. The response time is recorded. The idea is that a longer response time indicates an unconscious bias that exists around gender. If it takes an individual longer to respond to a picture of a woman as a scientist, then that person has an unconscious bias toward women and science. A less formal means to increase or sustain the number of women on campuses through hiring committees is to be intentional about the composition of the committee. While leaders such as department chairs and deans can take a primary role in convening a committee, other faculty can also volunteer and organize to shape committee composition. For example, faculty can organize to increase the women in a particular college or discipline by strategically placing faculty with a consciousness around gender issues on hiring committees.

We also recommend that community colleges engage in discussion and research to conduct a review of current work-life policies. Many current policies rely on the federal Family Medical Leave Act minimum (twelve weeks of unpaid leave) with the option of using sick time or disability benefits for additional time. Because community colleges typically have a sixteen-week semester time frame, the federal minimums are inadequate. Department chairs and colleagues are often forced to seek creative solutions when individuals need time off to manage unanticipated life events.

Surveys of faculty, reviews of progressive policies, and needs analysis are all important steps in developing new policies. Two trends within community colleges may aid in fostering flexibility: distance learning courses and compressed course schedules. Distance learning courses may be scheduled in time frames different from the sixteen-week norm; even if they are not, the flexibility of working from home may assist faculty in sustaining their workloads because they do not have to come to campus as often as if courses are face-to-face. Compressed course schedules, such as scheduling a semester-long course during the first or last eight weeks of a semester with double the meeting time for each session, also support flexible workload assignments.

Another method is to create an official advocacy group such as a women's commission or a faculty-led committee. Colleges that do not already have a chapter of the American Association of Women in Community Colleges might consider establishing one. This association, an affiliate of the American Association of Community Colleges, asserts it is "the leading national organization that champions women and maximizes their potential" (Association of Women in Community Colleges, 2004). Local chapters recruit from all employee sectors and provide opportunities for female faculty and administrators to learn together and mentor one another. Chapter meetings can serve as reasonable venues in which colleagues may engage in discussions about institutional policies, procedures, and practices that may have an impact on female faculty.

Conclusion

Women have long been attracted to community colleges, primarily due to the historical dominance of women in this sector and the perceptions of equity. Yet the entry of women into community colleges cannot be taken for granted. More and more colleges and universities are taking an interest in promoting women in male-dominated disciplines, primarily STEM fields, and placing increased emphasis on work-life balance practices. Community colleges may not be in competition for enrollment. Katsinas and Tollefson (2009) projected that community colleges will see higher enrollments in the next ten years due to an increase in the number of college-aged Americans looking for a low-cost postsecondary education. However, community colleges may see competition for women who become role models and mentors to students who seek degrees in STEM fields and other male-dominated vocational and technical fields. Although this chapter focuses on women, many of the recommendations apply to other groups that are historically underrepresented and disenfranchised in higher education. More work needs to be done that looks at masculinity with the same

NEW DIRECTIONS FOR COMMUNITY COLLEGES • DOI: 10.1002/cc

attention to disaggregating by discipline and addressing interpersonal dynamics.

References

American Association of Women in Community Colleges. "Mission Statement." Washington, D.C.: American Association of Women in Community Colleges, 2009. Retrieved Sept. 6, 2009, from http://www.aawccnatl.org/.

American Council on Education. *The American College President*. Washington, D.C.: American Council on Education, 2007.

American Federation of Teachers. *American Academic: The State of the Higher Education Workforce, 1997–2007*. Washington, D.C.: American Federation of Teachers, 2009. Retrieved Aug. 1, 2009 from http://www.aftface.org/index.php?option=contentandtask =viewandid=530.

Armenti, C. "May Babies and Posttenure Babies: Maternal Decisions of Women Professors." *Review of Higher Education*, 2004, 27(2), 211–231.

Cataldi, E., Fahimi, M., and Bradburn, E. M. *2004 National Study of Postsecondary Faculty (NSOPF:04): Report on Faculty and Instructional Staff in Fall 2003*. Washington, D.C.: U.S. Department of Education, Office of Educational Research and Improvement, 2005.

Drago, R., and others. "Bias Against Caregiving." *Academe*, 2005. Retrieved November 1, 2010, from http://www.aaup.org/AAUP/pubsres/academe/2005/SO/Feat/drag.htm

Grumet, M. *Bitter Milk: Women and Teaching*. Amherst: University of Massachusetts Press, 1988.

Hagedorn, L. S., ,and Laden, B. V. "Exploring the Climate for Women Community College Faculty." In J. Palmer (ed.), *Community College Faculty: Characteristics, Practices, and Challenges*. New Directions for Community Colleges, no. 118. San Francisco: Jossey-Bass, 2002.

Huber, M. T. *Community College Faculty Attitudes and Trends, 1997*. Stanford, Calif.: National Center for Postsecondary Improvement, Stanford University, 1998.

Kanter, R. M. *Men and Women of the Corporation*. New York: Basic Books, 1977.

Katsinas, S. G., and Tollefson, T. A. *Funding and Access Issues in Public Higher Education: A Community College Perspective. Findings from the 2009 Survey of the National Council of State Directors of Community College*. Tuscaloosa: Education Policy Center, University of Alabama, 2009.

Lester, J. "Performing Gender in the Workplace: Gender Socialization, Power, and Identity Among Female Faculty." *Community College Review*, 2008, 34(4), 277–305.

Lester, J. "Not Your Child's Playground: Workplace Bullying Among Community College Faculty." *Community College Journal of Research and Practice*, 2009, 33(5), 444–462.

Lester, J., and Lukas, S. "The Actors Behind the Curtain: Representation of Women Faculty in Community College Institutional Decision-Making." In J. Lester (ed.), *Gendered Perspective on Community Colleges*. New Directions for Community Colleges, no. 142. San Francisco: Jossey-Bass, 2008.

Mason, M. A., and Goulden, M. "Do Babies Matter (Part II)? Closing the Baby Gap." *Academe*, 2004, 90(6), 10–15.

National Center for Education Statistics. *Enrollment in Title IV Degree-Granting Two-Year Institution, by Gender and Discipline: Fall 2003*. Washington, D.C.: National Center for Education Statistics, 2009. Retrieved Aug. 10, 2009, from http://nces.ed.gov/dasolv2/tables/mainPage.asp?mode=NEWandfilenumber=49.

National League for Nursing. "Nursing Education Research." New York: National League for Nursing, 2009. Retrieved Sept. 4, 2009, from http://www.nln.org/research/slides/exec_summary.htm.

Obama, B. Excerpts of the President's Remarks in Warren, Mich., July 14, 2009. Retrieved Sept. 2, 2009, from http://www.whitehouse.gov/the_press_office/Excerpts-of-the-Presidents-remarks-in-Warren-Michigan-and-fact-sheet-on-the-American-Graduation-Initiative/.

Sallee, M. W. "Work and Family Balance: How Community College Faculty Cope." In J. Lester (ed.), *Gendered Perspective on Community Colleges*. New Directions for Community Colleges, no. 142. San Francisco: Jossey-Bass, 2008.

Starobin, S. S., and Laanan, F. S. "Broadening Female Participation in Science, Technology, Engineering, and Mathematics: Experiences at Community Colleges." In J. Lester (ed.), *Gendered Perspective on Community Colleges*. New Directions for Community Colleges, no. 142. San Francisco: Jossey-Bass, 2008.

Strouse, M., Ebbers, L. H., and King, A. R. "Hiring and Developing Quality Community College Faculty." *Community College Journal of Research and Practice*, 2008, *32*(12), 985–998.

Townsend, B. K., and LaPaglia, N. "Are We Marginalized Within Academe? Perceptions of Two-Year College Faculty." *Community College Review*, 2000, *28*(1), 41–48.

Ward, K., and Wolf-Wendel, L. "Fear Factor: How Safe Is It to Make Time for Family?" *Academe*, 2004, *90*(6), 28–31.

West, M. S., and Curtis, J. W. "AAUP Faculty Gender Equity Indicators, 2006." Washington, D.C.: American Association of University Professors, 2006.

Wolfe, J. R., and Strange, C. C. "Academic Life at the Franchise: Faculty Culture in a Rural Two-Year Branch Campus." *Review of Higher Education*, 2003, *26*(3), 343–362.

Wolf-Wendel, L., Ward, K., and Twombly, S. "Faculty Life at Community Colleges: The Perspective of Women with Children." *Community College Review*, 2007, *34*(4), 255–281.

Jaime Lester is an assistant professor of higher education in the College of Humanities and Social Science at George Mason University, Fairfax County, Virginia.

Trudy Bers is executive director of research, curriculum, and planning at Oakton Community College, Skokie, Illinois.

New Directions for Community Colleges • DOI: 10.1002/cc

6

*For the foreseeable future, community colleges must
seriously address hiring, retaining, and facilitating
upward mobility for faculty members. Moreover, they
should recruit a faculty corps that is more reflective of
both the students they serve and the demographics of their
college service area. It is critical for community colleges
to employ and retain a diverse faculty.*

Recruiting and Mentoring Minority Faculty Members

William Vega, Kenneth Yglesias, John P. Murray

> As a nation we have lost our more than century-long advantage in postsec-
> ondary educational attainment and are at risk of falling farther behind.
> S. Goldrick-Rab, D. N. Harris, C. Mazzeo, and G. Kienzl,
> "From Challenges to Opportunities" (2009)

The need to replace faculty, counselors, administrators, and student support staff within North American community colleges is evident. Current
literature indicates that 40 to 80 percent of community college faculty will
retire by 2015. In some states, such as California, the rate of academic and
student service administrators and college chief executive officer retirements exceeds 60 percent. Public community colleges have a larger percentage of faculty between the ages of forty-five and sixty-four and the
lowest percentage of faculty age sixty-five or older than any other segment
of higher education (McCormack, 2008). Data suggest that community college faculty and administrators tend to retire at or near the traditional
retirement age of sixty-five. Therefore, hiring and replacing the large body
of community college faculty and administrators through 2020 will likely
be both a daunting and problematic task for the nation's community colleges. Moreover, the economic, political, and sociocultural implications of
these efforts at replacement are multidimensional as community colleges
continue to evolve in diverse ways.

NEW DIRECTIONS FOR COMMUNITY COLLEGES, no. 152, Winter 2010 © 2010 Wiley Periodicals, Inc.
Published online in Wiley Online Library (wileyonlinelibrary.com) • DOI: 10.1002/cc.427

Diversity

During the foreseeable future, community colleges must seriously address hiring, retaining, and facilitating the upward mobility of faculty members. Moreover, the national community college movement should recruit a faculty corps that is reflective of both the students they serve and the demographics of their college service area. Springer and Westerhaus (2006) point out that "numerous studies and longstanding research show that a diverse faculty and student body lead to great benefits in education for all students." Moreover, employee diversity is socially responsible, and a critical component of a sustainable solution to the pending shortage of community college faculty.

Faculty Qualifications and Experiences

When seeking to employ a faculty member, community colleges need to determine what qualities they want in a teacher. The question of the skills that faculty need "is particularly important because ... there is currently little discussion ... of the skills necessary for those seeking to become community college faculty" (Townsend and Twombly, 2007, p. 33). Moreover, as Cejda explains in Chapter Four in this volume, very few individuals seek to prepare themselves for community college teaching positions. The minimum qualification in most disciplines is a master's degree from an accredited college or university. Our view is that it is also desirable that those seeking community college positions have experience at teaching, counseling, library media, or academic work at some level or recognized industry experience in the vocational and occupational fields found in community colleges. However, these experiences, coupled with a master's degree in the related area, are not the only qualifications a community college should consider. These are but a subset of the knowledge base needed to teach in a community college.

Given the current political and economic interests of national public policies, community colleges provide economic development, regional economic growth, and relevant workforce training. To achieve these ends, community colleges focus on course and program outcomes and local labor market trends. The faculty hired will need to be vested in the skills and components of academic disciplines relevant to employers. They need to be aware of the needs of employers, as well as understand macroeconomic policy and the missions of the local community college and its culture.

Therefore, hiring faculty with the right qualifications is only the first step toward building a diverse faculty. In order to secure the future of a diverse faculty, new faculty members need to be socialized to understand and embrace the multidimensional community college mission. Learning on the job may have worked in the 1950s, 1960s, or 1970s, but that option is now doomed to failure. We contend that most new community college faculty members are neither knowledgeable nor well informed about national, regional, or statewide community college policy; the college mission; the diversity of the student body; heavy teaching loads; and other relevant areas. Most new faculty are also unaware of the pedagogical demands of community college teaching, and it is equally important that they understand these demands if community colleges wish to retain them (Murray, 2007). Faculty will need to develop the necessary skill sets quickly and, in many cases, without the benefit of the senior faculty who shaped the community college these new faculty members will inherit.

Mentoring

> For decades, leadership in the faculty and administrative ranks has not been representative demographically of the communities and student bodies it serves. As U.S. demographics shift, filling employment voids on college campuses will offer institutions opportunities to examine their own values regarding diversity. This opportunity will allow colleges to provide professional development and training for new hires. Mentoring will be a key ingredient to their long-term success [Roueche, Richardson, Neal, and Roueche, 2008, p. 12].

Although mentoring for those interested in developing a successful career in community college teaching can be informal and casual, we favor a formal, structured mentoring program for lasting and sustainable action. This may include an internship and focuses on data-driven accountability.

Because there is often a paucity of faculty of color who can serve as mentors (Thomason, 2008), community colleges need to seek creative ways to attract and effectively mentor minority faculty. One creative method is to use e-mail (Single and Single, 2005) to connect a suitable mentor with the mentee. One such example of a structured e-mentoring program is described by first-year school principal, Sheryl Boris-Schacter (Boris-Schacter and Vonasek, 2009). Her local school superintendent arranged a mentorship program with an experienced and distinguished elementary school principal. The program consisted of e-mail mentoring, relationship development, and sustained and frequent communication between mentor and mentee. Respectful nurturing responses from the mentor, a communication tone characterized by caring, mutual support, playfulness, and regular face-to-face meetings over lunch, coffee, or dinner were additional components of the program. The program, through guided communication methodologies, enhanced the mentees' experiences and developed an understanding of the work, built a lifelong relationship, and promoted professional sustainability. The use of e-mail aided both mentor and mentee in expressing reciprocal caring, injecting humor into their work, and providing emotional and intellectual nurturance. A good source for creating an effective telementoring environment is found in the work of Bennett and others (1998).

The community college movement could benefit by developing or partnering with mentoring programs sponsored by universities, major professional organizations, or other public and nongovernmental agencies with characteristics similar to those found in business and public administration training programs. The programs in business and public administration usually pair a seasoned, mature, and experienced mentor with a distinguished record of executive service with the mentoring candidate.

Internship programs, providing real-world experience along with a designated mentor, have long been the staple of clinically oriented M.B.A. programs. Major international corporations such as Microsoft, Accenture, Deloitte, IBM, PricewaterhouseCoopers, Ernst and Young, Hewlett Packard, McKinsey and Company, and Capgemni have instituted internship and mentoring programs with such universities as New York University; San Jose State University; University of Southern California; University of California, Berkeley; University of Washington; University of Texas, Austin; Arizona State University; University of California, Los Angeles; University of Phoenix; and the University of Michigan. As a result of the internship experience, mentoring by seasoned professionals, and a quality business education program with many clinical opportunities, the nine corporations report hiring a number of new employees from the intern cohorts. Jobs are never guaranteed in these programs, but all sides agree that the exposure, work experiences, networking opportunities, and contacts with a professional mentor have yielded positive results for many of these M.B.A. students.

An example of such a program for community college personnel is the emerging online doctor of management in community college policy and administration at the University of Maryland. The program incorporates a team-based executive coaching component focused on leadership development. Several courses include individualized coaching or mentoring of each student in the areas of institutional assessment in the community college environment, advocacy and accountability, and organizational theory (University of Maryland University College, n.d.).

An alternative to mentoring for members of minority groups who are interested in developing a career in community college teaching is to identify an established educational program such as a university master's, doctoral, or post-master's certificate program that uses strong, well-developed mentoring components within the program offerings, course work, clinical experiences, or student internships.

For those interested in a community college faculty or administrator position, several universities have or are developing programs that include a mentoring component. Currently, programs of study at several California State Universities (Long Beach and Fullerton), the University of LaVerne, North Carolina State University, the University of Southern California, and the University of Texas integrate mentoring in their doctoral studies programs.

Components of a Formalized Mentoring Program

The list in this section attempts to formalize the mentoring that now occurs informally between experienced community college professionals and those interested in pursuing professional work in community colleges. These informal arrangements are often suggested through postgraduate course work, mutual friends, or the persistence of a potential mentee seeking out a community college sponsor. Sometimes a community college leader, senior faculty member, or long-time administrator identifies an interested potential mentee, and the relationship is established. We have multiple examples and much anecdotal evidence shared by colleagues and friends concerning experiences regarding informal mentoring relationships. We recognize the value of informal mentoring relationships. However, such relationships are often the result of favoritism and may foster the worst in the old-boy networks. Therefore, we believe that formalized and structured programs are necessary if community colleges are to live up to their full potential as institutions of higher and postsecondary education.

It is our view that an effective and sustainable, formalized mentoring program should include the following components:

- Specific goals of the mentoring program
- Outcomes of the program—objectives behaviorally articulated with expected outcomes
- Length of time of the program—approximate number of hours expected to be devoted to the mentoring experience on a weekly basis
- Mentor training—empathy, listening, communication skills, time commitment
- Clearly articulated descriptions of clinical or internship experiences associated with the program
- List of formal or informal course or workshop attendance that should be undertaken by mentees during the length of the program
- A well-developed tracking and data collection plan to assess the intended outcomes
- Anecdotal notes on each candidate by mentor, mentee, and program organizers
- Yearly surveys of mentees noting career or job changes as a result of being mentored

Conclusion

A formal mentoring project for minority faculty must be accountable and backed up with reliable data to have a systemic and sustainable effect

NEW DIRECTIONS FOR COMMUNITY COLLEGES • DOI: 10.1002/cc

over time. Successful mentoring for minority faculty and administrators must be:

- Credible
- Reliable
- Systemic and structured
- Highly regarded
- Focused on outcomes
- Associated with a credible organization or institution

Successful mentoring programs must evidence:

- Positive thinking among all participants
- A strong cohort of mentees and mentors
- Tracking and data collection to document success and failures
- Objectives documenting clinical or internship experiences
- Long-term analysis on the careers of mentees

A robust and informed mentoring program for minority faculty will include mentoring by a well-respected practitioner; job shadowing, clinical, or internship experiences; and time spent in the daily life and activities of the culture of the community college. If community college leaders fail to address the need for a more diverse faculty and do not establish or partner with a mentoring program, the more costly failures will be to the students, their education, and the communities the colleges serve.

References

Bennett, D., and others. "Critical Issues in the Design and Implementation of Telementoring Environments (New York, Center for Children and Technology)." 1998. Retrieved November 1, 2010, from http://www2.edc.org/CCT/admin/publications/report/ 09_1998.pdf.

Boris-Schacter, S., and Vonasek, G. "Dear Gayle, Dear Sheryl, Using E-Mail for a Principal Mentorship." *Phi Delta Kappan,* 2009, *90*(7), 490–494.

Goldrick-Rab, S., Harris, D. N., Mazzeo, C., and Kienzl, G. *Transforming America's Community Colleges: A Federal Policy Proposal to Expand Opportunity and Promote Economic Prosperity.* Washington, D.C.: Brookings Institute, 2009.

McCormack, E. "Community Colleges Hope to Keep Aging Professors in the Classroom." *Chronicle of Higher Education,* June 13,2008, p. A14.

Murray, J. P. "Rural Community College Faculty Satisfaction." In P. Eddy and J. P. Murray (eds.), *Rural Community Colleges: Teaching, Learning, and Leading in the Heartland.* New Directions for Community Colleges, no. 137. San Francisco: Jossey-Bass, 2007.

Roueche, J. E., Johnson, L. F., Roueche, S. D., and Associates. *Embracing the Tiger: The Effectiveness Debate and the Community College.* Washington, D.C.: Community College Press, 1997.

Roueche, J. E., Richardson, M. M., Neal, P. W., and Roueche, S. D. "From Challenges to Opportunities." In J. E. Roueche, M. M. Richardson, P. W. Neal, and S. D. Roueche (eds.), *The Creative Community College: Leading Through Innovation* (pp. 7–26). Washington, D.C.: Community College Press, 2008.

Springer, A., and Westerhaus, C. "How to Diversify the Faculty." 2006. Retrieved November 1, 2010 from http://www.aaup.org/AAUP/protect/legal/topics/howto-diversify.htm.

Single, P. B., & Single, R. M. "E-Mentoring for Social Equity: Review of Research to Inform Program Development." *Mentoring and Tutoring,* 2005, *13*(2), 301–320.

Thomason, C. O. "Recruitment, Retention, and Mentoring Faculty of Color: The Chronicle Continues." In N.V.N. Chism (ed.), *Faculty at the Margins.* New Directions for Higher Education, no. 143. San Francisco: Jossey-Bass, 2008.

Townsend, B. K., and Twombly, S. B. *Community College Faculty: Overlooked and Undervalued.* ASHE-ERIC Higher Education Report, no. 32–6. Hoboken, N.J.: Wiley, 2007.

University of Maryland University College. "Doctor of Management in Community College Policy and Administration." Retrieved Jan. 4, 2010, from https://www.umuc.edu/marketing/market663.shtml.

WILLIAM VEGA *is a former chancellor of the Coast Community College District, California, and is currently Distinguished Faculty in Residence, Department of Advanced Studies in Education and Counseling, California State University, Long Beach.*

KENNETH YGLESIAS *is a former chancellor of the Coast Community College District, California.*

JOHN P. MURRAY *is a professor in the Department of Advanced Studies in Education and Counseling, California State University, Long Beach.*

NEW DIRECTIONS FOR COMMUNITY COLLEGES • DOI: 10.1002/cc

7

The American community college has posed, for a period of time, some distinctively unique concerns pertaining to legal issues. However, the most pressing legal issues facing community colleges now are those regarding personnel.

Legal Concerns in Community College Employment Matters

Roy C. Rodriguez

The American community college has posed some distinctively unique concerns pertaining to legal issues. However, the most pressing legal issues facing community colleges today are those regarding personnel. The diversity of programs community colleges offer require that personnel (specifically faculty) come to the institution with a wide variety of educational backgrounds, experiences, and training.

Nationally, community colleges are in the throes of turnover in all areas of employment. Much has been written regarding turnover in the administrative ranks of these institutions. However, a greater number of professional and faculty employees will enter the community college in the near future , and a large percentage of these new employees will have little or no knowledge of the purpose and mission of the American community college.

Contracts and Employees

Evelyn (2001) has forecast a hiring boom for all level of employees in American community colleges during the early twenty-first century. What legal pitfalls exist for community colleges with this new surge in employment?

The contemporary public community college, like all other public institutions, has a vast array of employees. They range from high-level

New Directions for Community Colleges, no. 152, Winter 2010 © 2010 Wiley Periodicals, Inc.
Published online in Wiley Online Library (wileyonlinelibrary.com) • DOI: 10.1002/cc.428

administrators, faculty, professional level individuals, to classified levels. All have unique roles and responsibilities , and all connect the community college with some form of employment contract. The basic tenets of contract law still hold. Community colleges are held to the legal precedence that has given guidance for over fifty years.

The basic relationship between an employee and the community college is governed by contract law. Contracts may be written or oral, and even when there is no express contract, common law principles may allow the courts to imply a contract between the parties. Contracts may be very basic—for example, an offer letter from the college stating a position title and a wage or salary may, on acceptance, be construed to be a contract. Absent any writing, oral promises by a manager or supervisor may nevertheless be binding on the college through the application of agency law. A court may also look to the written policies of a college or its consistent past practices to imply a contract with certain employment guarantees. For these reasons, it is important that administrators and counsel ensure that communications to employees and applicants, whether written or oral, and the provisions in employee manuals or policies, clearly represent the institution's actual intent regarding the binding nature of its statements (Kaplin and Lee, 2006).

Contracts may take various forms even within an institution. In community colleges, particularly if the college has a tenure system, contracts may be governed by state statute or even by state civil service or personnel regulations. They may also be governed by the state's common law of contracts. In most community colleges, faculty contract provisions may be found in faculty handbooks, policy statements, or in the "academic custom and usage" doctrine through which courts seek to fill in gaps in written or implied contracts (Trower, 2000).

Community College Full-Time Faculty

A review of case law from 1980 to 2008 identified the vast majority of employee-versus-college litigation as pertaining to the role, scope, and functions of full-time community college instructors.

Community colleges commonly have written and published standards or criteria to guide decisions regarding faculty appointments, contract renewals, promotions, and the granting and termination of tenure. Since they often constitute the contract between the faculty member and the college (thus binding the college), such evaluative standards and criteria should receive the careful attention of administrators and faculty members alike. If particular standards are not intended to be legally binding or are not intended to apply to certain kinds of personnel decisions, those limitations should be made clear in the standards themselves.

While courts will enforce standards or criteria found to be part of the faculty contract, the law accords postsecondary institutions (including community colleges) wide discretion in determining the content and specificity of those standards and criteria. In *Lewis* v. *State of Oklahoma* (2002), the Tenth Federal Circuit found that Tulsa Community College was within its authority to ask faculty in certain areas of "high need" to participate in recruiting efforts as part of their evaluation. In addition, in *Llamas* v. *Butte Community College District* (2001), the Ninth Federal Circuit found that the California college could require all faculty to participate in various community organizations and functions. This activity was seen as part of the faculty's responsibilities as community college instructors. A similar decision was held by the Eleventh Federal Circuit in *Babb* v. *Lake City Community College* (1995). Once again, community college faculty were required to be active and visible in their service area in Florida as part of their yearly evaluations.

A variety of legal questions have been addressed by the courts regarding the responsibilities of community college instructors to their students, their colleagues, and the college. The courts have followed the standard established by *Brouillette* v. *Board of Directors of Merged Area IX* (1975). The Eighth Federal Circuit stated, "Such matters as the competence of teachers and the standards of its measurement are not matters of constitutional dimensions. They are peculiarly appropriate to state and local administrations" (p. 127). In *Law* v. *Board of Trustees of Dodge City Community College* (2009), the court upheld the dismissal of a tenured instructor who continued to receive poor teaching evaluations after the college had provided considerable assistance in this area. In *Thein* v. *Feather River Community College* (2008), the California court upheld the demotion of a tenured instructor who failed to meet with his students, dismissed classes inappropriately, and was argumentative with colleagues. Finally, in *Carpanzano* v. *College of Dupage* (2004), a federal district court in Illinois supported that the board of trustees has the legal authority to establish a code of ethics for community college instructors. The code of ethics these trustees established was not in violation of any collective bargaining agreements.

Community college trustees and administration need to clarify the scope, role, and purpose of faculty. If the institution's philosophy is such that faculty are required to perform duties above and beyond teaching and advising students, these duties need to be clearly stipulated. As instruction becomes more Web based, new issues regarding contact with students will arise. Will there be limitations on the number of Web-based courses taught by a faculty member? Will faculty need to maintain the same number of office hours? Will a faculty member be allowed to teach all of his or her courses over the Web? Will faculty be required to be knowledgeable of how to use technology for instruction? These are all issues that need to be addressed with legal counsel so that appropriate policies can be established.

Part-Time Faculty

Facing ever-increasing financial constraints, most community colleges have increasingly turned to part-time faculty to provide instruction. In 2004, 65 percent of the faculty at public community colleges, in contrast to 27.5 percent of the faculty at public four-year universities, taught part-time (Cohen and Brawer, 2006).

The questions being raised about part-time faculty involve such matters as pay scales, eligibility for fringe benefits, access to tenure, rights on dismissal or nonrenewal, and status for collective bargaining purposes. Each of these questions may be affected by two more general questions: (1) How is the distinction between a part-time and a full-time faculty member defined? (2) Are distinctions made between (or among) categories of part-time faculty members? Also important are state and federal statutes and administrative rulings on such matters as defining bargaining units for collective bargaining, retirement plans, civil service classifications, faculty tenure, wage and hour requirements, and unemployment compensation. These statutes and rulings may substantially affect what can and cannot be provided for in part-time faculty contracts.

In *Womack v. San Francisco Community College District* (2007), the plaintiff, a part-time instructor, stipulated that his actual working conditions exceeded the requirements of his part-time contract. His contentions were that the time he spent with students (teaching, advising, counseling, discussing assignments, and so on) were equivalent to well over the time of a full-time instructor. He taught three classes per quarter for the community college. He asked the court to declare that his employment was in fact a de facto full-time teaching position and he was therefore entitled to the salary and benefits of a full-time instructor. The California Court of Appeals did not agree with Womack. In its decision, the court stated:

> The definition of "full-time" varies from college to college, depending on the existence of unique programs and the outcomes of negotiations with individual faculty unions. A court-imposed definition, while establishing a uniform standard, would not likely consider all the factors at each college, and would result in immediate personnel problems for colleges with definitions that varied from a court-imposed definition [p. 20].

A similar decision was imposed by a federal district court in North Carolina. In *Jenkins v. Trustees of Sandhills Community College* (2003), the college decided not to hire Jenkins, a part-time instructor, for the coming semester. Jenkins, an African-American woman, contended that the college did not hire her as a part-time instructor because of her race and gender. She stated that a number of other part-time faculty were hired by the college during the same period. The court stated that Jenkins did not meet the standards for an equal protection violation by the college. Most important, the court stipulated that it could not impose its opinion on when or who the college should hire for temporary employment. The court stated that to impose its will on the ways and methods of hiring temporary employees would go "far beyond the scope and authority of this Court." In addition, the court stated that the trustees and administration of the college are "the best situated to understand the needs and interests of the college in any particular semester or year" (p. 432).

To respond effectively to issues involving part-time faculty, administrators should understand the differences in the legal status of part-time and full-time faculty members at their institutions. In consultation with counsel, they should make sure that the existing differences in status and any future changes are adequately expressed in part-time faculty contracts, along with any college rules and regulations. Administrators should also consider the extent and clarity of their institution's legal authority to maintain the existing differences if they are challenged or to change the legal status of part-timers if changes are advisable to effectuate new college policy.

Adverse Employment Decisions

Just as community college trustees are vested with the authority to hire, assign, promote, and grant tenure to employees, these same governing bodies may undertake adverse employment decisions against an employee. In the context of employee discipline, an adverse employment decision may include reprimand, suspension (with or without pay), demotion, nonrenewal, layoff, or dismissal for cause. Judicial review of an adverse employment decision involves a series of inquiries:

- Did the college comply with the contractual obligation to the employee?
- Were procedures for undertaking an adverse employment decision followed?
- Was substantial evidence provided in proof of the alleged facts justifying the adverse employment decision?
- Did the facts establish good cause under the terms of the contract or policy handbook?

For the most part, the courts recognize that some discretion must be afforded to the college in determining whether an adverse employment decision is warranted. Stress on overly detailed written criteria and unnecessarily literal interpretation of those criteria cannot be permitted to eliminate consideration of relevant but subjective factors in evaluating employees. Similarly, the courts are hesitant to substitute their judgment for the judgment and discretion properly exercised by the college administrators. For example, in *Allan* v. *Board of Trustees of Atlantic Community College* (2000), a New Jersey State Appeals Court affirmed a ruling that a president's reprimand of a tenured faculty member was consistent with the terms of the institution's policy handbook and made in good faith. Despite the fact that the president's decision contravened the recommendation of a review committee that proposed the reprimand be invalidated, the court held that the president's final determination sufficiently set forth job-related reasons for the adverse employment decision based on continued neglect of duties and supported by the record of poor yearly evaluations.

Unless employee misconduct is so egregious or extreme that a single instance would justify cause for dismissal, the range of adverse employment decisions permits a system of progressive discipline. Under such a system, an employee's single instance of misconduct might result in a written reprimand. If the behavior continues, an escalation of penalties, to include suspension or demotion, could be implemented. A documented pattern of continuing misconduct would result in dismissal. In *King v. Hawkeye Community College* (2000), an Iowa Court of Appeals reasoned that a record of progressive discipline effectively documented a history of repeated correction, counseling, and training of an employee about job-related deficiencies. In view of the evidence that the employee had not adequately conformed her conduct to the requirements of the job, the court found that dismissal was justified.

Dismissal of Employees.   The termination of an employee, including tenured faculty, is reliant on the long-established legal concept of adequate cause (Kaplin and Lee, 2006). Dismissal is possible only if the college can show demonstrated incompetence or dishonesty, manifest neglect of duty, or conduct that substantially impairs the individual's job-related responsibilities. Among the specific grounds that are often incorporated in institutional disciplinary policies, unprofessional conduct, insubordination, immorality, neglect of duty, and incompetence are typically identified (Beckham and Dagley, 2005). A discussion of some of the most-used causes for dismissal will indicate how they have been used in community colleges.

Unprofessional Conduct.   Unprofessional conduct includes a range of inappropriate behaviors. It may be implicated when an employee (including faculty) engages in lack of collegiality, harassment, refusal to heed prior warnings regarding inappropriate conduct, or excessive filing of grievances or complaints.

In *Clay v. Board of Trustees of Neosho County Community College* (1995), a tenured faculty member in Kansas was dismissed for "capricious disregard of accepted standards of professional conduct" (p. 770) based on instances of arbitrary treatment of students, rude and discourteous behavior to peers and staff, and insubordination toward supervisors. In response to complaints from students, faculty, and administrative personnel, the department chair initially substantiated the complaints and then met with the faculty member and identified problems that, if not corrected, would result in termination. When this approach failed, the chair recommended termination, and extensive due process procedures were set in motion. The faculty member received written notice of the charges against her, and a faculty committee began an inquiry that led to a finding of cause for dismissal. Following a formal hearing, a recommendation for dismissal was advanced to the board of trustees, which affirmed discharge. A federal district court in Kansas ruled that the charges were established by clear and convincing evidence and held that dismissal was justified because the faculty member had received repeated counseling, specific warnings, and reprimands about the behavior that ultimately led to her dismissal. This case is an excellent example of community college administrators who followed all the appropriate standards of law required for dismissal of an employee.

Neglect of Duty.   Neglect of duty involves repeated failure to perform duties prescribed by college policy (or state law) or to comply with reasonable directives or institutional policies relating to employee responsibilities. Instances of neglect of duty are often appropriate for a plan of progressive discipline. For example, an employee's persistent absenteeism would justify an initial warning, followed by a formal reprimand and heightened oversight to ensure compliance with directives. If the behavior continues, the documented evidence of excessive absenteeism would constitute "good and sufficient reason" to suspend without pay or demote, and future instances might justify termination (Beckham and Dagley, 2005).

Repeated warnings, coupled with persistent directives, were illustrated in *Hood* v. *Compton Community College District* (2005). A long-term nursing instructor in California challenged her dismissal for "significant neglect of duty" (p. 954). The record established that the instructor had been relieved of her teaching assignments and directed to develop two new introductory courses for nursing. However, the instructor did not develop syllabi and other materials for these courses and ignored requests for the submission of these materials. When the instructor left the college, without informing supervisors, for a lengthy stay in Florida, she was repeatedly contacted by college officials, advised that she was absent without permission, and directed to report immediately and complete her assignments. On her return, she submitted no written materials related to the task of developing the two new courses. The California Court of Appeals found that the college had provided a clear and convincing record that the nursing instructor's dismissal was warranted. The *Hood* case is a good example that displays that the burden of proof is on the institution to compile documentary evidence showing the court that all charges against the employee are true and accurate.

Immoral Conduct.   Allegations of immorality (moral turpitude) involve conduct sufficiently egregious and notorious to bring the individual concerned or the community college into public disgrace or disrespect. In many cases, the immoral conduct would be so extreme that a single instance is sufficient for dismissal. Factors to be weighed in assessing a basis for immorality as a cause for dismissal would include (1) the likelihood of recurrence of the questioned conduct; (2) the extenuating or aggravating circumstances, if any; (3) the effect of notoriety and publicity; (4) any impairment of teacher-student relationships; (5) a disruption of the educational process; (6) motive; and (7) the proximity or remoteness in time of the conduct (*Morrison v. State Board of Education*, 1969).

When the employee is a faculty member, documenting immoral conduct will often require demonstrating a nexus between the behavior and the individual's fitness to continue his or her professional responsibilities. The requirement for nexus is intended to balance the instructor's right to privacy against the interest of the institution in ensuring efficiency and realizing its mission as a community college. In *Board of Directors of Des Moines Area Community College v. Simons* (1992), the instructor's misdemeanor conviction for possession of marijuana and cocaine and her actions in allowing drug sales to take place in her home provided just cause for dismissal. As in most other cases of this type, once the arrest became public, the Iowa college suspended the instructor with pay pending the outcome of the criminal trial. In the college's administrative hearing, it was determined by extensive testimony that the instructor's effectiveness was substantially impaired. The board's review of testimony from other faculty and its conclusion that the instructor's conduct directly contradicted her teaching role as a psychologist preparing students for careers in drug counseling were significant factors on which the court relied in affirming dismissal.

Professional Competency.   Employee competency is associated with the ability of the employee to perform job responsibilities as described in the institutional handbook or position descriptions. For example, an instructor's competency may be determined by his or her effectiveness in the classroom, knowledge of subject matter, or willingness to adapt to new teaching techniques. When dismissal for incompetence is implicated, it involves a pattern of behavior, and the institution must provide the necessary documentation to support the cause. An important dimension of documentation is observation and evaluation of performance, an activity that is increasingly mandated by policy in all community colleges. In *Cotter v. Trustees of Pensacola Jr. College* (1989), low student evaluations, testimony concerning student complaints, high withdrawal rates, low student enrollments in the instructor's classes, and repeated efforts by superiors to improve the instructor's performance were documented to warrant the adverse employment decision.

Incompetence involves job-related performance that falls below an acceptable standard and typically includes a remedial opportunity to correct deficiencies if those deficiencies do not pose a significant and immediate risk of harm to students or compromise close working relationships with colleagues. When employee competency is at issue, progressive discipline is replaced by the identification of performance deficiencies, assistance to correct deficiencies, a reasonable opportunity for remediation, and assessment of whether performance has improved (*Nelson* v. *Pima Community College District*, 1996).

In documenting lack of professional competency, evaluation systems must yield a documentary record that confirms the fairness and reasonableness of the process, complies with legal mandates, and meets the test of substantial evidence. Unsubstantiated claims of inadequate performance, conflicting appraisals of performance, or lack of uniform standards in the evaluation process may contribute to the view that the evidence to support an adverse employment decision is insufficient. Competent and substantial evidence, which may include classroom observations, student evaluations or complaints, testimony of colleagues, anecdotal memoranda, or a combination of sources will sustain the legitimacy of the process and justify an adverse employment decision (*West Valley–Mission College* v. *Concepcion*, 1993).

Proper notice of deficiencies and time in which to correct those deficiencies conforms to essential requirements of due process and helps rebut claims that the evaluation system is arbitrary or capricious. This concept is best illustrated in *Spanner* v. *Rancho Santiago Community College District* (2004). The California Court of Appeals noted that the college provided formal and informal notification to the employee (a guidance counselor) of specific deficiencies in his performance over a four-year period. Periodic evaluations established that the employee did not improve his performance, and letters, memoranda, and oral warnings to the counselor described how his performance was deficient, using language congruent with that later used in the formal charges involving lack of competence. This documentation was persuasive in convincing the court that the employee had adequate notice of the standard of performance required, sustaining dismissal.

Constructive Discharge

Beginning in the latter part of the 1990s, a new form of dismissal litigation began to appear that the courts have deemed "constructive discharge." Constructive discharged is defined by the courts as a condition constructed by the employer that makes the employee's work environment so intolerable that the employee resigns (*Katz* v. *Georgetown University*, 2001). Claims of constructive discharge are evaluated under a reasonable-person standard by most state and federal courts. It is not sufficient to assert that working conditions are difficult or unpleasant. The former employee must seek to establish that working conditions were so intolerable that a reasonable person would feel compelled to resign. In other words, given the conditions, a reasonable person in the same or similar circumstances as that of the employee would have no other choice than to quit (*Cable* v. *Ivy Tech State College*, 1999).

NEW DIRECTIONS FOR COMMUNITY COLLEGES • DOI: 10.1002/cc

Two instructive cases involving constructive discharge give some guidance to community college instructors. The first is *Fertally* v. *Miami-Dade Community College* (1995). Miami-Dade is a multicampus community college district. Fertally, a full-time instructor, asserted that he was forced to quit his job as an instructor because the college district "forced" him to teach in three of the district's campuses, which caused him undue hardship and stress. He said that if he had refused to teach in the three campuses, the district would reduce his salary and possibly dismiss him from employment. Fertally was one of a handful of instructors required to teach at various campuses in the Miami-Dade service area. The Appeals Court of Florida agreed with Fertally's claim. Since the vast majority of full-time faculty in the Miami-Dade district taught at only one campus, asking Fertally to teach at three campuses was deemed as establishing an "intolerable work environment" (p. 1246).

The second case is *Lowell* v. *Asnuntuck Community College* (2003). Lowell, a full-time building trades instructor at Asnuntuck Community College in Connecticut, was reassigned to the welding shop trade program and the automotive mechanics program after a reduction in force of building trades faculty. Lowell claimed that this transfer of instructional duties was intolerable and placed him in a situation where he was forced to teach materials in which he was not trained. Therefore, he resigned his teaching position. The Superior Court of Connecticut agreed with Lowell. The court reasoned that although Lowell was capable of learning the new trade areas, it was "unreasonable" to require him to do so in order to maintain his job. The court stated that Lowell's position was tantamount to placing him in position where he could fail. Thus, the claim of constructive discharge was upheld, and the college was required to pay damages.

Due Process

Minimal constitutional standards required of community colleges (all public higher education institutions) when dismissal of a long-term employee (including tenured faculty) is contemplated would involve notice of the cause for dismissal, notice of the names of witnesses and their testimony, meaningful opportunity to be heard, and an impartial panel with appropriate expertise. Other protections extended to an employee may include allowing objections to any prospective hearing panel member permitting cross-examination of witnesses and providing opportunities for the presentation of testimony and evidence on the employees' behalf. The right to have representation by an attorney in a termination decision will often depend on the law of the particular jurisdiction. However, the right to counsel is relatively standard for most termination hearings (Perritt, 1992).

The best advice to college administrators is to ensure that a sound and minimally adequate pre-termination hearing is provided to employees who have protected property interests in continued employment in order to avoid future litigation of that due process issue. In *Lockhart* v. *Cedar Rapids Community College District* (1998), the Supreme Court of Iowa ruled that the college had given Lockhart, an untenured instructor, more than adequate due process even though Lockhart did not have a property right to employment. The college had offered him an opportunity to speak on his behalf before a review board. Lockhart refused the offer, stating that the members of the board were prejudiced against him. The court stated that the college's sole responsibility was to provide the opportunity.

In *Nini* v. *Mercer County Community College* (2009), Nini, a seventy-year-old custodian for the New Jersey college, was terminated for failure to perform his duties. Nini claimed that his termination was due to his age. The college displayed clear evidence that Nini was performing his custodial responsibilities poorly, was absent on many occasions, was discourteous to staff and students, and refused to attend training. He was given ample notice of his deficiencies regarding job performance and two pre-termination hearings. The Supreme Court of New Jersey found for the college. In its ruling, the court stated that Mercer College "was fully aware of Nini's age and physical conditions . . . every effort was made to provide assistance to Nini in order for him to perform his responsibilities in the manner required by . . . policy" (p. 547).

Conclusion

Community colleges are experiencing major employment turnover. As this new generation of employees enters community colleges, administrators will be making significant decisions. The coming generation of employees is technologically aware. Individuals from support level to faculty are comfortable and eager to use technology. In addition, many employment decisions are being made with the assistance of technology. More and more colleges (and other public employers) are using Internet search methods to screen the background of applicants or finalists. What factor will this technological factor make in personnel decisions for the future? What legal issues will this infusion of technology bring to community colleges? We do not know. However, technology is but one concept that the past generation of administration did not face.

The next generation of employees will be more transitional. They have lived in various communities and are more willing to move to other communities than the current generation of employees (Twenge, 2006). Historically community college employees have come from the community, lived in the community for many years, and plan to stay in the community. As the more mobile generation enters the community college, will this pose some legal concerns for the institution? Once again, we do not know.

Although the level of judicial scrutiny applicable to community college employment decisions will vary, the courts are unlikely to interfere when the employment decision is based on criteria reasonably related to job requirements, free of impermissible discrimination or the denial of a constitutional right to speech or association, reached by proper procedures, and supported by substantial evidence. Judicial intervention would necessitate review of a host of factors that most community colleges use to make employment decisions, a role courts have neither the competency nor the resources to undertake.

Sound employment practices provide a record of events, incidents, appraisals, discussions, interviews, admonitions, and directives that can be relied on to support the evidentiary sufficiency and credibility of an employment decision. When efforts to correct or improve an employee's performance have failed and an adverse employment decision is compelled, that decision must be predicated on standards reasonably related to job requirements and substantial adherence to the procedural requirements established by law, contract, collective agreement, and institutional policy.

Development and implementation of legally sound employment practices and procedures will not eliminate legal disputes but should yield a documentary record that substantiates the fairness and reasonableness of the process, establishes the proper predicate for an adverse employment decision, and elaborates the procedural integrity of the process. Community colleges need to review their contacts and handbooks periodically. Are these instruments reflecting the changing dynamics of the employee characteristics and traits? Similarly, evaluation procedures, especially those for faculty, need to be closely reviewed. Technology is now part of the classroom. How technologically aware should the next generation of faculty be? Is this a fair requirement? Are faculty who teach online evaluated the same as those in a classroom setting? What about the courses? Do online courses hold the same level of rigor or expectations as face-to-face instruction? If not, are we in the precarious position of having little or no guidance on legal issues that might arise in this area?

Community college administration, trustees, and legal counsel must have these discussions before they are forced to enter the judicial system because of an employee's legal action against the college.

References

Allan v. Board of Trustees of Atlantic Community College. U.S. Dist. LEXIS 2329. 2000.
Babb v. Lake City Community College. U.S. App. LEXIS 27891. 1995.
Beckham, J., and Dagley, D. *Contemporary Issues in Higher Education Law.* Dayton, Ohio: Education Law Association, 2005.
Board of Directors of Des Moines Area Community College v. Simons. 493 N.W.2d 879. 1992.
Brouillette v. Board of Directors of Merged Area IX. 519 F.2d 126. 1975.
Cable v. Ivy Tech State College. 200 F.3d 467. 1999.
Carpanzano v. College of Dupage. U.S. Dist. LEXIS 2381. 2004.
Clay v. Board of Trustees of Neosho County Community College, Kansas. U.S. Dist. LEXIS 4071. 1995.

Cohen, A. M., and Brawer, F. B. *The American Community College.* (5th ed.) San Francisco: Jossey-Bass, 2006.
Cotter v. Trustees of Pensacola Jr. College. 548 So. 2d 731. 1989.
Evelyn, J. "The Hiring Boom at Two Year Colleges." *Chronicle of Higher Education,* June 15, 2001, pp. A8-A9.
Fertally v. Miami-Dade Community College. 651 So. 2d 1283. 1995.
Hood v. Compton Community College District. 26 Cal. Rptr. 3d 180. 2005.
Jenkins v. Trustees of Sandhills Community College. 259 F. Supp. 2d 432. 2003.
Kaplin, W. A., and Lee, B. A. *The Law of Higher Education.* (4th ed.) San Francisco: Jossey-Bass, 2006.
Katz v. Georgetown University. 246 Fed. 3d 685. 2001.
King v. Hawkeye Community College. U.S. Dist. LEXIS 1695. 2000.
Law v. Board of Trustee of Dodge City Community College. U.S. Dist. LEXIS 30899. 2009.
Lewis v. State of Oklahoma. U.S. App. LEXIS 12687. 2002.
Llamas v. Butte Community College District. U.S. App. LEXIS 3882. 2001.
Lockhart v. Cedar Rapids Community School District. 577 N.W.2d 845. 1998.
Lowell v. Asnuntuck Community College. Conn. Super. LEXIS 2344. 2003.
Morrison v. State Board of Education. 461 P.2d 375. 1969.
Nelson v. Pima Community College. 83 F.3d 1075. Decided May 7, 1996.
Nini v. Mercer County Community College. 406 N.J. Super. 547. 2009.
Perritt, H. H. *Employee Dismissal Law and Practice.* Hoboken, N.J.: Wiley, 1992.
Spanner v. Rancho Santiago Community College District. 119 Cal. App. 4th 584. 2004
Thein v. Feather River Community College. U.S. Dist. LEXIS 108357. 2008.
Trower, C. A. *Policies on Faculty Appointments: Standard Practices and Unusual Arrangements.* San Francisco: Jossey-Bass/Anker, 2000.
Twenge, J. M. *Generation Me.* New York: Free Press, 2006.
West Valley–Mission College v. Concepcion. 16 Cal. App. 4th 1766. 1993.
Womack v. San Francisco Community College District. 384 Cal. App. 4th 891. 2007.

ROY C. RODRIGUEZ *is a professor of higher education administration at Texas Tech University.*

8

Community colleges must ensure that the hiring process reflects the desired outcome by first defining student success and then allowing the definition and description to guide all steps of the hiring process while avoiding pitfalls along the way.

Hiring for Student Success: A Perspective from Community College Presidents

Marie Foster Gnage, Kevin E. Drumm

Great organizations are made up of great people. And for leaders at all levels within those organizations, the ability to find, hire, integrate, and retain great people is an absolutely critical skill—critical to their organization's success, and critical to their own success. But for most people, making great appointments is difficult, time-consuming, and even scary.

Claudio Fernandez Araoz, *Great People Decisions* (2007)

For anyone who followed the appointment proceedings for Supreme Court Justice Sonja Sotomayor, the nature of that historic hire was instructive, including her own rulings on the legality of hiring procedures for public organizations. It is instructive for college hiring processes even though few play out in such a highly public political theater. The process of hiring for student success is, indeed, as important as "hiring" a Supreme Court Justice: college staff, faculty, and administrators affect the lives of students daily and help to determine their success in college and in life.

What is at stake is student success and its infrastructure: the quality of the academic environment, the quality of learning, and services for students, all of which contribute to students' achievement of their education goals. Therefore, it is vital to keep the focus on what the candidate can contribute to the success of students.

Hiring Concerns. General responses to questions about hiring can be found in numerous books and articles devoted to the hiring process.

NEW DIRECTIONS FOR COMMUNITY COLLEGES, no. 152, Winter 2010 © 2010 Wiley Periodicals, Inc.
Published online in Wiley Online Library (wileyonlinelibrary.com) • DOI: 10.1002/cc.429

Colleges have made projects out of getting it right—that is, ensuring that the process yields the best new employee. The *Chronicle of Higher Education* has developed an online newsletter on hiring. The most in-depth discussion of hiring in community colleges—thirty winning strategies for hiring—is Jones-Kauvalier and Flannigan's *The Hiring Game: Reshaping Community College Practices.*

Most senior college leaders, indeed managers of any complex enterprise, have made great hiring decisions but also some that are subpar. What distinguishes the two outcomes? The answer can only be that in successful hiring, the end determined the means: the desired positive outcome was given serious consideration throughout the hiring process. For community colleges, the emphasis should always be on hiring faculty, staff, and administrators who are committed to student success in word and deed. How many times have we seen a search with a political or loyalty end in mind, or another objective for the hiring process that might have pushed student success to a second priority–or pushed it out of the hiring equation altogether?

Our national higher education periodicals are replete with stories of hiring gone bad, stories of institutions falling victim to many of the pitfalls of hiring. Riggs (2009) recently wrote specifically about the faulty filling of administrative vacancies, listing

> "job hoppers" with "flashy credentials, excellent interview skills . . . [and] a pattern of hopping from job to job"; the "internal 'safe' candidate" who is usually a "dedicated employee . . . [lacking] in qualifications and skills for the position but 'they know how we do things around here'"; and the "retirement spiker" who wants the job because it will increase his/her retirement earnings [p. 3].

Weekly newspaper headlines yield specific examples: a fired instructor sues the college that questioned the legitimacy of a degree he indicated he earned; a professor is fired for an improper relationship with a student who died; a faculty member reaches financial settlement over a dismissal resulting from teaching style; a faculty member is fired for enrollment fraud; and an instructor sues the college for a firing that resulted from the faculty member's display of offensive or offending cartoons. Not all problems with faculty and staff are necessarily the result of ineffective hiring practices, but some are. Understanding searches that did go wrong can be instructive: mistakes might have been avoided if hiring authorities had made student success paramount throughout the entire hiring continuum, including discontinuation if necessary.

Hiring for Student Success.   Begin with the end in mind: the goal is to employ faculty, staff, and administrators who understand and demonstrate the necessary practices for student success. Institutions should begin with ensuring an institutional understanding and definition of student success as a start to the hiring process—before the job description or the advertisement. Student success should be reflected in the college's mission statement, vision, and strategic plan and should guide the development of a meaningful job description and, of course, the entire hiring process. The following initiatives and best practices may help define student success:

- Achieving the Dream initiatives help more community college students succeed. An institution's investment is a commitment to broad institutional change informed by student data in order to help students complete courses, advance from remedial to credit courses, complete gatekeeper courses, be retained from one semester to the next, and earn certificates and degrees.
- Programs funded by Title III, TRIO, and Title IV focus on the improvement of academic programs and student outcomes: retention and graduation rates and institutional management that support the success of disadvantaged students.
- Results of the Community College Survey of Student Engagement show that the more actively engaged students are with college faculty and staff, other students, and the subject matter, the more likely they are to learn and achieve their academic goals.
- Other student success programs—first-year experience, developmental education, campus compact, and national community college benchmarking project—are all focused on helping students to be successful.

Every community college desires to offer the best opportunities and practices possible for effective learning and successful student outcomes. Taking the necessary steps to thoughtfully analyze the meaning as well as the best practices for realizing success helps in the evaluation of what one wishes to achieve with a specific hiring decision. McClenney and Waiwaiole (2005) write:

> Community colleges are known for opening the door to the masses for higher education. An open door, however, is not enough. Meeting the needs of community college students and helping them to reach their educational goals is a daunting task. It's one that requires strategic thinking, relentless focus, and deliberate action. … Then comes the crucial work of purposefully re-designing learning experiences and support services that will engage and challenge these diverse students to complete their educational goals [p. 38].

Recognizing the importance of these student success objectives and using the six strategies that follow are major steps toward purposefully developing a process that yields employees committed to student success outcomes.

- What do you wish to achieve with the hire?
- Do you need to complete a team?
- Do you want change to occur in policies, procedures, processes, or attitudes—a change agent?
- Is program development important?
- Do you want to increase recruitment?
- Do you want an increase in retention, graduation, transfer—student outcomes?
- Do you want all of the above?

Another consideration in writing the job description is a recognition of who is being served or who needs to be served: high school students, recent high school graduates, adults, veterans, minority students, African American and/or Latino males, speakers of English as a second language, students with disabilities, underprepared students, dislocated workers. Cramer and Prentice-Dunn (2007) note that "young adults entering college confront a myriad of social, academic, and psychological challenges" (p. 771). A majority of students entering community colleges face myriad challenges, often far beyond what a university first-year student typically faces. Individuals working in community colleges must be able to address all of these challenges. Regardless of the job description, the ability to serve a diverse population has to be a requirement even when a particular job focus may be limited to a specific population.

Smith and Moreno (2006) ask, "Will myths remain excuses?" (p. 64). They indicate that increasing the diversity of faculty members and administrators continues as a high priority but is slow in happening in part because of the myth that African American, Latina/o, and American Indian prospective faculty members are being drawn to high-paying jobs in industry. Diversity must be a consideration in the hiring process. Think of the role that a diverse faculty and staff play in creating a college environment conducive to encouraging student success through role modeling, mentoring, and carrying out their assigned duties while guiding students toward the completion of educational goals. Research supports the value of a diverse faculty and staff. Do keep in mind the legal landscape and the ramifications of diversity as the only criteria.

Perhaps this is the point at which we emphasize that all jobs at community colleges are important to student success, from the newest entry-level staff member to the highest-level administrators and the president. What happens when those who take care of college facilities do not understand or care about the learning environment: the cleanliness and orderliness of classrooms and labs, the maintenance of facilities, the appearance of the physical learning environment and the signals that gives? What happens if campus police or public safety officers are hired who do not understand that the college is not the mean streets of the city? What happens when newly hired staff want to be physically cordoned

NEW DIRECTIONS FOR COMMUNITY COLLEGES • DOI: 10.1002/cc

off from the students they must serve? What happens if faculty are hired who want to teach only bright students at certain times of the day in certain delivery modes? What of the librarian who still thinks that libraries are for books and quiet only? What happens if an administrator's concern is for job security rather than advocacy and support of students? The hiring process should be used to weed out individuals who do not come to the college to support students in the achievement of their educational goals. Zeiss (2004) notes that "recruiting excellent employees is the most important skill of good leaders" (p. 16). We would insert "commitment to student success" into Zeiss's important declaration.

Developing a job description is not as simple as cutting and pasting from another institution's Web site simply because it includes a seemingly complete list of duties deemed sufficient to draw appropriate candidates. Certainly there are day-to-day duties that are common to similar positions at all community colleges. The issue becomes how to ascertain that a job description and the ad are descriptive of a specific job opportunity that will lead to the hiring of the best person for the position. Attracting the right people requires ensuring that the job description is written so that prospective candidates will understand the requirements and so that those who will be working with the new colleague understand the relationship of that person's position to their own. Therefore, the position description should be clearly written. It must define expectations and communicate responsibilities in line with the college's direction. CPS Human Resource Services adapted a list of key components of an effective job description from Michael Zwell's *Creating a Culture of Competence* (2000). An adaptation of CPS's list follows:

- *Job purpose*: A one-sentence description of the overall purpose or mission of the job that provides the rationale for why the job exists and how it contributes to the college. Its effectiveness can be measured by how well it reinforces for employees the critical role the position plays in the organization's success. Do not despair if it takes more than one sentence; the goal is conciseness and clarity.
- *Goals and objectives:* Somewhat broad and general statements about what incumbents should be accomplishing—that is, key criteria for setting performance objectives. The goals and objectives are opportunities to emphasize the importance of mission, vision, values, and student success. If indeed the person is expected to be a change agent, develop policies that could change the culture within the institution, be the cheerleader, and provide leadership for ensuring that student success is engrained in the culture of the institution, that information should be made explicit.
- *Reporting relationships:* The title of the position to which the incumbent reports and the titles of jobs reporting to it. The search committee or

the hiring supervisor should be prepared to talk about the duties and responsibilities of those who report to the position.

- *Duties and responsibilities:* The duties and responsibilities of the position written as simply yet completely as possible, with the caveat that the list of duties is not meant to be exhaustive—that is, there will be other duties as assigned. This is where it is made clear that "that's not my job" is an unacceptable attitude and response because it does not support student success.
- *Key technical skills and knowledge:* The important technical and professional skills and knowledge required to do the job for the selection process and the professional development process. Given rapidly changing technology and tech-savvy students, it will be important to emphasize the criticality of being open to learning and using new technology skills. Technical skills and knowledge should reflect both existing and future needs.
- *Key success factors:* Brief descriptions of the key behaviors and abilities that are critical to achieving the position's mission and goals. It is important for faculty and staff to have a picture of success. *Performance measures*: The measures of how well the job is being performed and how accomplishment of the goals and objectives of the position can be measured.
- *Competency model:* The competencies *identified for the position* that differentiate superior and satisfactory performance.
- *Job fit:* The factors within the job that certain employees may find particularly satisfying or dissatisfying, such as a heavy volume of paperwork, travel, and a diverse student population.
- *Career pathways:* Opportunities for other positions at the college after serving in this role.

A well-written job description makes the remainder of the hiring process less susceptible to glitches. It provides a blueprint for candidates, the search committee, and the hiring supervisor. Perhaps this blueprint will serve to dissuade those who think that they can do the job even though they lack the credentials. Furthermore, if past practices have been questionable—for example, hiring based on personal preferences rather than qualifications—this will also taint the recruitment process where a clear advertisement, job description, and fair search will serve to unmuddy the waters. Then, too, the search committee may have to look beyond their ideal candidate—quite often someone like them.

The job description's value begins in the compensation and benefits office as determination is being made about salary or salary range, while the job description continues to be important well after the position is filled: both the supervisor and the employee can review it to make sure that they are on course. Often the job description is a foundation for annual performance reviews, so it is crucial to get it right from the beginning. If there is conflict or grievance, the job description becomes a point of reference for the senior administrator, mediator, or arbitrator to make critical personnel decisions. Experts note that an effective job description contains the necessary detail that the downstream processes will require without containing so much detail that it needs to be frequently rewritten.

A good job description makes writing the advertisement less challenging. The goal of an advertisement for the position is not to attract just any candidate, but the right candidate. Therefore, it is important to accurately describe the job and its requirements, as well as the benefits of working at your institution with your students. Start the ad with what is key. The ad should reference the job description and the Web site where a full description may be found, describe the college, and clearly communicate the core requirements. More and more community colleges, in maximizing their marketing and recruitment dollars, write ads that include only the job opening, the college information, and the Web site address for more information. This makes it quite opportune to provide more information that not only attracts a candidate but attracts the right candidate with a briefer and less expensive but nevertheless attractive advertisement.

The Role of the Search Committee.   After carefully defining the position and the characteristics sought in a hire, selection of a strong search committee may be the most critical decision an executive makes, especially because highly important decisions are being delegated to a committee, even if the final candidate is not their call, but a recommendation. The search committee is a group of employees responsible for selecting candidates for interviewing candidates and recommending candidates for hire. Some colleges have established protocols for choosing members of such committees; others choose volunteers. Populating committees with volunteers is taking a chance that the committee will be made up of a group that is not diverse in its broadest sense or by members who have their own agendas. What is not desirable is a committee that is composed of people looking for someone just like themselves. If the committee is representative of diverse groups, then there is greater chance of diversity of thought and evaluation of candidates. For example, a search for a faculty member or academic or student affairs staff should include not just academic and student affairs representatives on the committee but also someone from business services, or information and technology, or facilities and grounds, or possibly students. These members certainly change the complexion of the discussion.

It is important to clearly communicate the rules of engagement and the charge to the committee, along with parameters for the search, that it recommend candidates who are committed to student success. Committee members must receive training in conducting committee business so that the charge means something to them. Training can be conducted by human resources or by another responsible office to ensure that the legal do's and don'ts are understood. Search committee members should strongly support the college's mission, vision, values, and strategic priorities that are the guideposts of student success. They may see different interpretations and means of achieving these key institutional goals; this is to be expected and perhaps even welcomed. The eventual new employee will have to work with those holding differing opinions and perspectives. It is a plus for a new employee to be exposed to a variety of perspectives during the selection process.

Every college has someone who works with committees on what not to ask candidates during an interview. However, greater emphasis should be placed on the important questions to ask. Interviewers must clearly define institutional mission, and interviewees must be able to clearly discuss personal values. Search committee members must let the job description, not personal preferences, be the focal point of the interview. They must present questions and evaluate responses to determine a candidate's commitment to college philosophy and mission, to open access and a diverse student body that requires multiple learning and support strategies, to using best practices and developing best practices, and to a philosophy of enhancing and supporting students' experiences from initial enrollment through completion of educational goals. Generally interview question types include self-awareness, career awareness, technical skills, hypothetical, and behavioral—questions that allow the committee to make sure that the person can really "walk the talk."

Background Checks and Unexpected Pitfalls. Leave no stone unturned in ensuring that the candidate's credentials and evidence of experience is supported by references and background checks. More than one news story has resulted when a successful candidate was identified on his or her first day, or later, as having been previously employed at an institution not listed on the application or résumé. Employment at the other institution was not listed either because it ended in forced resignation or firing. While Google seems to have risen in popularity as a means of finding secret lives and actions, the surest way is still to be thorough in checking references and ask questions such as, "If given the opportunity, would you hire this person for this position at your institution?" There are still colleges that do not check references, which is shocking considering the dangers. The common excuse is that nobody wants to give any information for fear of lawsuits. You wouldn't bring strangers into your own home to work with or around your children without checking them out, so why would you allow one to work in your college with your students? A good practice is to let the candidate know that you may choose to call additional references. A candidate's objection may be a red flag.

Sometimes even after all other steps are taken conscientiously, pitfalls remain. There will be those who are not open to hiring anyone who is not from the community or of a particular persuasion. The common phrase is, "He [or she] is 'not a good fit.'" There is the internal candidate who is presumed to have paid his or her dues. There is the adjunct who has taught at the college for many years. Remember that you established the guidelines and parameters with student success in mind and that you are looking for the qualified person who demonstrates the attitude and attributes in the job description and posting. If politics rears its somewhat unattractive head as you approach a hiring decision, as it often does, do the right thing for students and let the hiring process as it was designed recommend the selection.

Even in cases where the hiring process is conducted by the hiring supervisor, it is important to ensure that student success is at the heart of the decision. A CEO may be hiring an executive assistant or chief of staff, and in these highly specialized and personalized positions, the importance of student success may take a back seat. But it should not. Even a chief external relations officer must focus ultimately on student success or risk that external politics will get in the way of such success.

After They Are Hired.   The support after hiring should be a component of the overall hiring process. Orientation to the college and the job is critical. Mentoring is highly encouraged, even by someone in addition to the immediate supervisor. Supporting the new employee's professional development is also critical, and probably at no other time is it more critical than shortly after hiring. Send the new employee to a workshop or institute in the area of expertise or to a national conference in his or her field. Forward articles that relate to the job. Review the job description early after hiring and ask if there are any questions or concerns. Repeat the review.

Here is what is at stake in the hiring process:

- The quality of the academic environment
- The quality of learning
- Meaningfulness of services for students
- Students' achievement of their education goals—from retention to graduation

Michael Zwell (2000) writes, "From the body of competency research to date, a basic set of six competencies differentiate the top quartile of performers from the rest in most positions in an organization: initiative, influence, results orientation, teamwork, service orientation, and, concern for quality" (p. 55). These competencies, combined with a commitment to student success, should be the decision factors in hiring. When this is the case, college administrators demonstrate their commitment to student success in both the hiring process and the hiring outcome.

References

CPS Human Resource Services. "Workforce Planning Tool Kit: Gap Closing Strategies." Washington, D.C.: CPS Human Resource Services, Dec. 1, 2007.

Cramer, R. J., and Prentice-Dunn, S. "Caring for the Whole Person: Guidelines for Advancing Undergraduate Mentorship." *College Student Journal,* 2007, *41*(4), 771–778.

Jones-Kavalier, B. and Flannigan, S. L. *The Hiring Game: Reshaping Community College Practices.* Washington, D.C.: American Association of Community Colleges, 2008.

McClenney, K., and Waiwaiole, E. "Focus on Student Retention: Promising Practices in Community Colleges." *Community Colllege Journal,* 2005, 75(6), 36–41.

Riggs, J. "Leadership, Change, and the Future of Community Colleges." *Academic Leadership.* 2009. Retrieved November 1, 2010, from http://www.academicleadership.org/emprical_research/581.shtml.

Smith, D. G., and Moreno, J. F. "Hiring the Next Generation of Professors: Will Myths Remain Excuses?" *Chronicle of Higher Education,* September 29, 2006, p. 22.

Zeiss, T. "Attracting, Developing, and Retaining Peak Performers: A Mandate for America's Community Colleges." *Community College Journal,* Feb.-Mar. 2004, pp. 14–17.

Zwell, M. *Creating a Culture of Competence.* Hoboken, N.J.: Wiley, 2000.

Marie Foster Gnage is president of West Virginia University at Parkersburg.

Kevin E. Drumm is president of Northern Wyoming Community College District.

New Directions for Community Colleges • DOI: 10.1002/cc

Community colleges across the United States are experiencing an extraordinarily high demand for new instructors. Institutions must make sound, long-term decisions by selecting candidates who honor the community college's past while heralding its future.

Now Hiring: The Faculty of the Future

Donald W. Green, Kathleen Ciez-Volz

On the first day of the semester, twenty-five students eagerly await their freshman composition instructor's arrival. A glance around the classroom reveals a wide array of differences among the students. Blacks, whites, Latinas/os, and Asians all populate the classroom. A dually enrolled high school student chats with a grandmother in her fifties. Some students busily text and tweet their friends; others have never sent an e-mail. At least two students speak English as a second or other language, and one individual has a documented learning disability. Some students have arrived academically prepared for college-level writing, yet many have only recently completed developmental course work designed to prepare them for the rigor of the general education curriculum. Still others will require long hours of tutoring, mentoring, and student-teacher conferences to learn to write proficiently.

Such diversity is the norm at America's community colleges, which, as open-door institutions, serve the most widely varied group of students in higher education. The community college teacher who enters that freshman composition class must know more than her discipline; she must possess the ability to engage and encourage, motivate and inspire, teach and learn from her diverse students. To educate learners with vastly different backgrounds, abilities, and levels of academic preparedness, community colleges need the best teachers available in the academic labor market. Hiring exemplary instructors is at once an educational and an economic imperative, for the typical "community college spends over $3 million on the career of one faculty member" (Flannigan, Jones, and Moore, 2004,

New Directions for Community Colleges, no. 152, Winter 2010 © 2010 Wiley Periodicals, Inc.
Published online in Wiley Online Library (wileyonlinelibrary.com) • DOI: 10.1002/cc.430

p. 826; J. Hammons, personal communication, August 1, 2008). Because nearly three-fourths (72 percent) of community colleges offer tenure (Twombly and Townsend, 2008), hiring one faculty member, who could hold her position for thirty years or more, is a long-term institutional commitment.

In the current social milieu, parents, legislators, policymakers, members of business and industry, and other institutional stakeholders demand accountability for student learning. Community colleges must therefore ensure that newly hired faculty members are both "a good fit" and a "valuable long-term investment" for the institution (Flannigan, Jones, and Moore, 2004, p. 827). Who are the community college teachers of the future? What qualities must they possess? How can academic administrators attract and retain them? "How," Flannigan, Jones, and Moore query, "will community college hiring practices ensure that new faculty members are able to appreciate the culture of the past while at the same time embrace the vision of the future?" (p. 824). By exploring the answers to these questions, stakeholders will gain insights into hiring the community college faculty of the future.

The Demand for Community College Faculty

Community college faculty members play a significant role among the professoriate in U.S. higher education (Twombly, 2005). Citing the *Chronicle of Higher Education's* 2005 *Almanac*, Twombly and Townsend (2008) report that as of the fall 2003 semester, community college professors were 43 percent of all the full- and part-time faculty members in public, nonprofit postsecondary institutions. The nearly 112,000 full-time faculty members employed by community colleges (U.S. Department of Education, 2007) represent one-fifth of all faculty members in U.S. higher educational institutions (Twombly, 2005). Community college instructors, moreover, teach approximately 37 percent of undergraduates—a figure that includes nearly 50 percent of all freshmen and sophomores (Twombly and Townsend, 2008). Given their impact on higher education, community colleges and their faculty certainly merit scholarly attention (Twombly and Townsend, 2008).

Throughout its history, the community college has based its mission on providing educational access and opportunity to all interested citizens. Unlike the mission of traditional colleges and universities, that of the community college concerns not the generation but rather the transmission of knowledge (Twombly and Townsend, 2008). Through university transfer and workforce development programs, the community college enables individuals to expand their personal and professional lives.

Since its inception, the community college has focused on teaching and learning as opposed to research. Characterizing "teaching" as the "hallmark" of community colleges, Cohen and Brawer (2003) remark that faculty members' "primary responsibility is to teach"; "rarely" do they "conduct research or scholarly inquiry" (pp. 76, 97). Because of the vast number of retirements now and for the foreseeable future at community colleges, a pressing demand for new faculty now exists. As Murray (1999) predicted, the first decade of the twenty-first century has provided exciting and challenging opportunities for community college leaders to "influence their institutions' futures by hiring the largest cohort of faculty employed at one time since the 1960s." Hired in the 1960s and 1970s, many community college faculty members have recently retired or are planning to do so in the near future. Indeed, the community college professoriate has long been graying, as illustrated by statistics from the U.S. Department of Education (2005): approximately 36 percent of faculty members are younger than forty-four years of age; 32 percent are between forty-five and fifty-four years old; 22 percent are between fifty-five and sixty-four years old; and 8 percent are sixty-five or older (cited in Twombly and Townsend, 2008). McCormack (2008) notes that community colleges employ a larger percentage of professors between forty-five and sixty-four years of age than does any other type of postsecondary institution. By 2003, this figure included nearly two-thirds of the community college professoriate, revealing the critical need to attract new instructors.

Not since their heydays in the 1960s and 1970s have community colleges experienced such a demand for faculty. To meet the "changing needs of the community college system" while undergoing a "significant hiring wave," institutions must develop "new perspectives on hiring practices" (Flannigan, Jones, and Moore, 2004, p. 835). As community college faculty retire in droves, leaders are tasked with recruiting, hiring, and retaining teachers who feel passionately committed to the community college mission of providing access and promoting success, embrace change, and enjoy teaching and learning in a multicultural environment. The faculty hired today will influence the direction of community colleges for generations to come; thus, community colleges must approach the hiring process with foresight and vision. Faced with increasing demands for accountability and shrinking budgets, these institutions must continue to perform some of the most complex tasks in higher education—tasks that range from remediating academically underprepared students to offering baccalaureate degrees in high-demand areas such as emergency nursing and early childhood education. Without doubt, community colleges need teachers equal to the challenges that lie ahead.

The Academic Labor Market

Central to the topic of hiring faculty is the concept of academic labor markets, which consist of "a supply of potential faculty members, colleges and universities that employ them, and various practices that govern the allocation of faculty to jobs." For "academic labor markets to function effectively and efficiently," both community colleges and prospective faculty members should understand an institution's definition of "quality faculty" as well as its hiring processes (Twombly, 2005, p. 424). Obtaining a community college faculty position is not usually high on the list of desired jobs, perhaps because two-year institutions enjoy significantly less positive press and prestige than do their four-year counterparts. Rarely does one hear a child exclaim, "I want to be a professor [let alone a community college professor] when I grow up!" Often instructors begin teaching at a community college by happenstance or even serendipity, as we did. Such a career path is not atypical. As Evelyn (2001) remarks, many individuals in the academic labor market "stumble upon the route" of teaching at a community college rather than steer their careers toward it.

Prior to teaching in community colleges, numerous instructors have held positions in other arenas, such as business and industry, K-12 schools, and four-year colleges and universities (Twombly and Townsend, 2008). Twombly (2005) views the community college labor market as "the center of a web of markets that has links to 4-year markets as well as to public schools and to various occupational markets" (p. 445). Woven from many professional threads, community colleges—now more than ever before— must attract exemplary faculty members. In the words of Twombly and Townsend, "There is no question that, to produce good learning outcomes, community colleges must employ effective faculty members" (p. 20). Efforts at hiring and retaining candidates should focus on their "expertise, talent, [and] skills," as well as "institutional and departmental require- ments" (Smith and Moreno, 2006). Selection committees must ask and answer pivotal questions before initiating the screening process:

- What qualities comprise excellence in teaching?
- What are the most important qualities of faculty members at this institution?
- How do we identify these qualities in candidates?

To make effective and efficient hiring decisions, search committees must reach consensus about the qualities that teachers at their institutions should have. Flannigan, Jones, and Moore (2004), however, contend that too many hiring committees neither fully understand nor clearly define the "important qualities that faculty must possess" (p. 826). Without a set of mutually agreed-on criteria, committee members may struggle to select the ideal candidate.

The Qualities of Exemplary Teachers

We compiled the following list, which is not exhaustive, of qualities of exemplary teachers and teaching from some of the literature (Polk, 2006; Stemler, Elliott, Grigorenko, and Sternberg, 2006; Helterbran, 2008; Walls, Nardi, von Minden, and Hoffman, 2002):

- Intelligent and knowledgeable about the discipline
- Distinguished by strong social and interpersonal skills
- Ability to communicate knowledge in "a meaningful, engaging manner" (Helterbran, 2006, p. 130)
- "Organized, prepared, and clear" (Walls, Nardi, von Minden, and Hoffman, 2002, p. 45)
- Enthusiastic about teaching
- Respectful and welcoming of diverse peoples and views
- Warm, open, and accessible to students
- Committed to lifelong learning
- Creative
- Flexible
- Caring and empathetic
- Humorous
- Skilled at creating an emotional environment in which students feel comfortable taking intellectual risks
- Cooperative and collegial
- Encouraging and motivational

The learner-centered teachers whose qualities are depicted on this list celebrate the mission of serving diverse students. Before reviewing applications, the committee should define these qualities and discuss their significance to the selection process. The committee must also clarify how it will identify these qualities in the candidates—for example, through the curriculum vita, an interview, a teaching demonstration, a teaching portfolio, reference checks, and the like. By agreeing on the qualities that it values in prospective faculty and the methods for assessing these qualities, the committee will increase its chances of making a positive hiring decision.

Through their seven principles for good practice in undergraduate education, Chickering and Gamson (1987) provide additional insights into effective instruction, which encompasses student-to-teacher and student-to-student interaction, the use of active learning techniques, and prompt feedback in response to questions, assignments, and assessments. Emphasizing time on task, successful teachers communicate high expectations for their students, whose diverse talents and learning styles they respect. Murray (1999) notes that Chickering and Gamson do not address content mastery or organizational abilities, perhaps because an instructor's expertise in these areas is assumed. Certainly command over one's subject matter is essential to sound instruction, yet a teacher's ability to communicate such knowledge through a variety of pedagogical approaches may be even more critical.

A capable teacher knows more than her discipline. She knows how to build relationships with students as she mentors and motivates, guides and inspires them. As Evelyn (2001) remarks, "simply lecturing" will not suffice in the community college classroom, where teachers must be able to apply their understanding of learning and motivation theory. Dedicated to lifelong learning, an excellent teacher remains open to exploring new pedagogies to reach students who differ in race/ethnicity, age, and levels of academic preparedness. Sensitive to her students' diverse learning styles, she varies her teaching approaches, experimenting with visual, auditory, kinesthetic, and reading and writing activities. Such teachers exist, but a persistent question remains: Where and how can community college leaders find them?

The Hiring Process for Community College Faculty

The process for recruiting and selecting effective community college faculty members remains a relatively neglected area of scholarly inquiry (Twombly and Townsend, 2008). Having surveyed the literature, Flannigan, Jones, and Moore (2004) conclude that little has been written about the hiring of community college faculty over the past fifty years. Similarly, Twombly (2005) remarks that a gap in the research exists about "how and where community colleges recruit faculty or what values and practices influence the hiring process" (p. 426). Conspicuously absent in the literature is information about how community colleges search for and select faculty members. That Flannigan, Jones, and Moore feel both "concerned and intrigued" by the paucity of scholarly books and articles compels other researchers and practitioners to explore the topic further (2004, p. 826). To address this concern, Twombly (2005) conducted a case study in which she investigated the values, policies, and practices that govern the faculty hiring process at various community colleges. Her definitions of these terms provide a useful framework for examining the selection process

- Values—important principles in defining "quality faculty"
- Policies—written guidelines that shape the hiring process
- Practice—a regularly instituted activity, such as a required teaching presentation

Only by agreeing on core values, reviewing policies, and implementing standardized practices can committees conduct effective searches.

Just as recruiting skilled athletes represents the "single most essential ingredient" in a successful college athletics program, so also does recruiting talented faculty form the foundation for a "first-rate academic department" (Olson, 2007, online only). The search process, remarks Olson, is an institution's "one opportunity to assemble the ideal team." To achieve academic excellence, Olson says, institutions must recruit, hire, and retain excellent faculty; the search process therefore represents one of the "most consequential tasks" performed on campus. Hiring exemplary faculty members entails the following steps:

NEW DIRECTIONS FOR COMMUNITY COLLEGES • DOI: 10.1002/cc

- Establishing the hiring committee
- Writing job descriptions and requirements
- Specifying qualifications
- Advertising the position
- Selecting individuals from the candidate pool
- Prescreening the semifinalists
- Interviewing the finalists
- Conducting reference checks (Murray, 1999).

Similarly, Flannigan, Jones, and Moore (2004) summarize the faculty hiring process in terms of an announcement of a position, a review of the applications, an interview protocol, and a selection of the leading candidate. Like Murray, Olson (2007) maintains that a successful hiring process begins with a selection committee that clearly understands its role: finding and choosing the best candidate after having determined the guiding values, policies, and practices. Once established, the committee must compose an advertisement that will attract applicants. As the institution's first communication with prospective instructors, the advertisement should clarify the college's mission and values while setting the stage for the ensuing process.

The interview traditionally represents the crux of this process. Flannigan, Jones, and Moore (2004), however, observe that both search committees and scholars have commented on the ineffectiveness of the interview model, which often fails to provide the depth necessary to determine the fit between the interviewee and the institution. Flannigan, Jones, and Moore further note that although the time-honored approach of crafting job descriptions and conducting interviews may lead to the hiring of a faculty member who is competent in her discipline, such an approach does not ensure that the new hire "possesses the ingenuity and passion needed to transcend traditional modes of instruction and provide new avenues for engaging community college students in the learning process" (pp. 824–825). Perhaps a deeper exploration of the hiring process will help committees evaluate a candidate's fit within the institution more effectively.

Several researchers have commented on the significance of *fit*—a term that merits closer examination. According to Murray (1999), the word *fit* implies that the candidate is well suited to both the position and the institution. Credentials alone rarely reveal an individual's abilities or indicate the fit between a prospective faculty member and the hiring institution (Flannigan, Jones, and Moore, 2004). Flannigan, Jones, and Moore maintain that a screening committee can assess fit by examining the compatibility of an applicant's values with those of the institution. Therefore, the committee must communicate the college's mission and values, as well as obtain information about the candidate's values. Twombly (2005) explains that *fit* refers to a candidate's sharing of the community college mission, knowledge of the service area, collegiality, and willingness to fulfill one's job responsibilities.

To determine fit more effectively, screening committees might develop an interview protocol with questions intended to elicit behavioral responses in terms of the candidate's previous experiences (Murray, 1999). Unfortunately, though, most selection committees do not undergo training regarding the use of interview questions to obtain the information necessary for making the best faculty selections (Flannigan, Jones, and Moore, 2004). Rather than present exclusively hypothetical scenarios about what a candidate might do if, say, a student could not attend class because of a conflict with work or child care, the committee might question the candidate about what she has previously done in such a circumstance. Interviewers will acquire a richer understanding of the candidate by posing behavioral questions, such as, "What did you do?" instead of, "What would you do?" These questions allow interviewers to gauge "how the candidate learns from mistakes, resolves conflicts, and solves problems" (Murray, 1999, p. 45).

Like the interview, a required teaching demonstration can play a pivotal role in the faculty hiring process. While admittedly a somewhat contrived process in which the candidate teaches before a jury of peers as opposed to a group of students in a real classroom setting, this exercise enables the committee to gain deeper insights into the candidate's teaching philosophy, persona, and practices. To assess the candidate's performance, the committee might consider using a rubric (an example is in the chapter appendix). This tool is admittedly limited in its usefulness because of the committee's brief observational period, yet it may provide a helpful approach for measuring the interviewee's teaching performance. Based on Chickering and Gamson's research (1987), this rubric focuses on teaching behaviors. While completing the rubric, the committee might raise questions whose answers it deems important indicators of effective practice—for example:

- Does the candidate exemplify qualities desired by the committee?
- Which of the seven practices emphasized by Chickering and Gamson does she apply?
- Do those practices support the college's mission? If yes, in what ways? If no, why not?
- Does the candidate appear to fit into the department and institution? If yes, in what ways? If no, why not?

Certainly a candidate's fit cannot be measured with an instrument alone but must also be determined intuitively—viscerally even. Perhaps, though, the approach outlined here will prove helpful during the hiring process.

To learn more about a candidate's teaching skills, committees might consider requiring a "first-day essay," like that to which Twombly (2005) refers. In such an essay, candidates explain the activities that they would conduct on the first day of class—arguably the most important day of the term. This essay could shed new light on an applicant's teaching philosophies and practices. Hiring committees might also ask finalists to share a teaching portfolio consisting of a syllabus, lessons, activities, assignments, and assessments, as Twombly observed at one college during her case study. A portfolio, whether in a printed or digital format, provides a more in-depth exploration of a candidate's approach to curriculum development, instructional design, and assessment, thus enabling the committee to assess fit more effectively. Such practices, when combined with the traditional interview, might facilitate the decision-making process for hiring committees.

The Influence of Technology on the Student-Teacher Dynamic

No discussion about hiring future faculty can be complete without addressing the influence of technology on the student-teacher dynamic. A survey of the literature reveals that advances in technology, coupled with those in learning and motivation theory, have dramatically influenced the roles of faculty and students and will continue to do so in the foreseeable future. For generations, the lecture has been the predominant form of instructional delivery on college campuses. Yet as Berge (2008) observes, "an educational system that has changed little for the past 150 years" often fails to engage digital natives—those individuals born after 1980—who are accustomed to multitasking, online social networking, gaming, and manipulating avatars in "metaverses" (p. 408). Able to access "multiple paths to content" through sundry electronic devices, today's students expect learning to be "fast-paced," "interactive," and rich in the use of multimedia (p. 408). Indeed, students and teachers alike live in a knowledge-based society filled with readily available content. Never before have humans been able to retrieve so much information so readily, as a Google search of virtually any term will illustrate. Because the sociocultural context of higher education has significantly changed, so also must community college instruction. Unlike in days of yore, instructors are no longer the "sole or major information source"; rather, their role has evolved to that of "facilitator, coach, or mentor" responsible for providing "leadership and wisdom in guiding student learning" (Berge, 2008, pp. 408–409). By harnessing the power of technology, teachers must at once individualize the learning experience for their students and build the academic social networks so vital to success and retention.

In the 1990s, the major paradigmatic shift in higher education entailed the creation of interactive online courses and the concomitant transition from a teacher-centric to a learner-centric model of instruction. For the past several years, higher educational researchers and practitioners have investigated the value proposition of hybrid or blended courses, which combine face-to-face and online instruction (El Mansour and Mupinga, 2007). As Berge (2008) reports, instructors have recently begun exploring the possibilities of three-dimensional "virtual worlds for at least some of their teaching and learning experiences," thus affording students a "venue for social networking, collaboration, and learning" within multiuser virtual environments like Second Life (pp. 408–409).

Without doubt, the future will offer many other exciting, innovative educational technologies. Ultimately, though, it is not technology itself that forms the foundation for effective community college teaching but rather the commitment of faculty to remain lifelong learners who foster in their students a perpetual desire for knowledge and understanding. The faculty of the future, like the students they teach, must continuously adapt to and influence change (Ciez-Volz, 2009), paving ever new directions for community colleges.

Conclusion

The teacher who enters the first-year composition class—or any other class, for that matter—on the first day of the semester at a community college must be among the most capable instructors in higher education, for she must perform many complex tasks on a daily basis. Possessing a desire to teach and a love for students, the community college teacher of the future must know her content well. She must understand learning and motivation theories. She must be "committed to working with and empowering students with widely diverse backgrounds, motivations, work habits, and goals" (Murray, 1999, p. 46). She must be prepared to work within an educational environment in which institutions, states, regional accrediting agencies, and other stakeholders are calling for accountability in the form of common standards, measurements, and ongoing improvement processes. And to meet the demands of the many digital natives in her classroom, she must be—or be willing to become—technologically proficient. She must be a facilitator skilled at creating active, collaborative experiences that enable students to learn from one another and, in so doing, to learn about themselves. She must understand that the need to be "social" is "fundamental" to an understanding of "the human condition" (Gazzaniga, 2008, p. 112). Most of all, she must understand that as inherently social beings, people want and need to interact with other people, and she must apply this understanding by building cooperative, constructivist learning experiences that facilitate human interaction.

This teacher is likely to be employed in a tenure-track position for potentially up to thirty years. Thus, the hiring institution will be making a nearly $3 million investment in her. It is incumbent on the institution to make a sound, long-term decision by selecting a candidate who honors the community college's past while heralding the future. As colleges continue to experience a flood of faculty retirements, they will need to hire a large cadre of instructors. By clarifying their values, policies, and practices, as Twombly (2005) urges, institutions can design a process for making more effective and efficient hiring decisions—decisions about the community college faculty of the future.

Appendix: Effective Classroom Practices Based on Chickering and Gamson's Research (1987)

Directions: For each indicator of effective teaching practice, please select a level that best reflects the candidate's performance. Then tally the points for each level of achievement to obtain the subtotals. Finally, add the subtotals to determine the total score.

Indicators of Effective Teaching Practice	*Levels of Achievement*				
	Exemplary (4)	Proficient (3)	Marginal (2)	Unacceptable (1)	Not Observed (0)
Student-to-teacher interaction					
Student-to-student interaction					
The use of active learning techniques					
Prompt feedback					
An emphasis of time on task					
The communication of high expectations					
Respect for diverse talents					
Subtotal for each level					
Total score					

References

Berge, Z. L. "Changing Instructor's Roles in Virtual Worlds." *Quarterly Review of Distance Education,* 2008, 9(4), 407–414.

Chickering, A. W., and Gamson, Z. F. "Seven Principles for Good Practice in Undergraduate Education." 1987. Retrieved July 29, 2008, from http://www.csuhayward.edu/wasc/pdfs/End percent20Note.pdf.

Ciez-Volz, K. "Currents of Change: The SIRIUS Initiative at Florida Community College." *Vicissitude: A Refereed Journal for College Leaders,* 2009, 1(1), 18–19.

Cohen, A. M., and Brawer, F. B. *The American Community College.* (4th ed.) San Francisco: Jossey-Bass, 2003.

El Mansour, B., and Mupinga, D. M. "Students' Positive and Negative Experiences in Hybrid and Online Classes." *College Student Journal,* 2007, 41(1), 242–248.

Evelyn, J. "The Hiring Boom at Two-Year Colleges." *Chronicle of Higher Education,* June 15, 2001, pp. A8–A9.

Flannigan, S., Jones, B. R., and Moore, W. "An Exploration of Faculty Hiring Practices in Community Colleges." *Community College Journal of Research and Practice,* 2004, 28, 823–836.

Gazzaniga, M. S. *Human: The Science Behind What Makes Us Human.* New York: Harper-Collins, 2008.

Helterbran, V. R. "The Ideal Professor: Student Perceptions of Effective Instructor Practices, Attitudes, and Skills." *Education,* 2008, *129*(1), 125–138.

McCormack, E. "Community Colleges Hope to Keep Aging Professors in the Classroom." *Chronicle of Higher Education,* 2008, *54*(40), A14.

Murray, J. P. "Interviewing to Hire Competent Community College Faculty." *Community College Review,* 1999, *27*(1), 41–56.

Olson, G. A. "Don't Just Search, Recruit." *Chronicle of Higher Education,* May 25, 2007. Retrieved July 29, 2008, from the Professional Development Collection database.

Polk, J. A. "Traits of Effective Teachers." *Arts Education Policy Review,* 2006, *107*(4), 23–29.

Smith, D. G., and Moreno, J. F. "Hiring the Next Generation of Professors: Will Myths Remain Excuses?" *Chronicle of Higher Education,* Sept. 6, 2006, p. B22.

Stemler, S. E., Elliott, J. G., Grigorenko, E. L., and Sternberg, R. J. "There's More to Teaching Than Instruction: Seven Strategies for Dealing with the Practical Side of Teaching." *Educational Studies,* 2006, *32*(1), 101–118.

Twombly, S. "Values, Policies, and Practices Affecting the Hiring Process for Full-Time Arts and Sciences Faculty in Community Colleges." *Journal of Higher Education,* 2005, 76(4), 423–447.

Twombly, S., and Townsend, B. K. "Community College Faculty: What We Know and Need to Know." *Community College Review,* 2008, *36*(1), 5–24.

U.S. Department of Education. (2007). *Digest of Education Statistics: 2007.* 2007. Retrieved Aug. 5, 2008, from http://nces.ed.gov/programs/digest/d07/tables/dt07_235.asp?referrer=report

Walls, R. T., Nardi, A. H., von Minden, A. M., and Hoffman, N. "The Characteristics of Effective and Ineffective Teachers." *Teacher Education Quarterly,* 2002, *29*(1), 39–48.

DONALD W. GREEN *is the executive vice president for instruction and student services at Florida State College at Jacksonville.*

KATHLEEN CIEZ-VOLZ *is the director of program development at Florida State College at Jacksonville's Kent Campus.*

NEW DIRECTIONS FOR COMMUNITY COLLEGES • DOI: 10.1002/cc

INDEX

Statement of Ownership

Statement of Ownership, Management, and Circulation (required by 39 U.S.C. 3685), filed on OCTOBER 1,2010 for NEW DIRECTIONS FOR COMMUNITY COLLEGES (Publication No. 0194-3081), published Quarterly at Wiley Subscription Services, Inc., at Jossey-Bass, 989 Market St., San Francisco, CA 94103.

The names and complete mailing addresses of the Publisher, Editor, and Managing Editor are: Publisher, Wiley Subscription Services Inc., A Wiley Company at San Francisco, 989 Market St., San Francisco, CA 94103-1741; Editor, Arthur M. Cohen, Eric Clearinghouse for Community Colleges, 3051 Moore Hall, Box 95121, Los Angeles, CA 90095; Managing Editor, Gabriel Jones, NDCC/CSCC, c/o UCLA Graduate School of Education, 2128 Moore Hall, Box 95121, Los Angeles, CA 90095-1521.

NEW DIRECTIONS FOR COMMUNITY COLLEGES is a publication owned by Wiley Subscription Services, Inc.. The known bondholders, mortgagees, and other security holders owning or holding 1% or more of total amount of bonds, mortgages, or other securities are (see list).

	Average No. Copies Each Issue During Preceding 12 Months	No. Copies of Single Issue Published Nearest To Filing Date (Summer 2010)
15a. Total number of copies (net press run)	1,307	1,156
15b. Legitimate paid and/or requested distribution (by mail and outside mail)		
15b(1). Individual paid/requested mail subscriptions stated on PS form 3541 (include direct written request from recipient, telemarketing, and Internet requests from recipient, paid subscriptions including nominal rate subscriptions, advertiser's proof copies, and exchange copies)	538	499
15b(2). Copies requested by employers for distribution to employees by name or position, stated on PS form 3541	0	0
15b(3). Sales through dealers and carriers, street vendors, counter sales, and other paid or requested distribution outside USPS	0	0
15b(4). Requested copies distributed by other mail classes through USPS	0	0
15c. Total paid and/or requested circulation (sum of 15b(1), (2), (3), and (4))	538	499
15d. Nonrequested distribution (by mail and outside mail)		
15d(1). Outside county nonrequested copies stated on PS form 3541	127	127
15d(2). In-county nonrequested copies stated on PS form 3541	0	0
15d(3). Nonrequested copies distributed through the USPS by other classes of mail	0	0
15d(4). Nonrequested copies distributed outside the mail	0	0
15e. Total nonrequested distribution (sum of 15d(1), (2), (3), and (4))	127	127
15f. Total distribution (sum of 15c and 15e)	665	626
15g. Copies not distributed	642	530
15h. Total (sum of 15f and 15g)	1,307	1,156
15i. Percent paid and/or requested circulation (15c divided by 15f times 100)	81.2%	79.7%

I certify that all information furnished on this form is true and complete. I understand that anyone who furnishes false or misleading information on this form or who omits material or information requested on this form may be subject to criminal sanctions (including fines and imprisonment) and/or civil sanctions (including civil penalties).

(signed) Susan E. Lewis, VP & Publisher-Periodicals

NEW DIRECTIONS FOR COMMUNITY COLLEGE

ORDER FORM SUBSCRIPTION AND SINGLE ISSUES

DISCOUNTED BACK ISSUES:

Use this form to receive 20% off all back issues of *New Directions for Community College*.
All single issues priced at **$23.20** (normally $29.00)

TITLE	ISSUE NO.	ISBN
_____	_____	_____
_____	_____	_____
_____	_____	_____

Call 888-378-2537 or see mailing instructions below. When calling, mention the promotional code JBNND
to receive your discount. For a complete list of issues, please visit www.josseybass.com/go/ndcc

SUBSCRIPTIONS: (1 YEAR, 4 ISSUES)

☐ New Order   ☐ Renewal

U.S.   ☐ Individual: $89   ☐ Institutional: $259
Canada/Mexico   ☐ Individual: $89   ☐ Institutional: $299
All Others   ☐ Individual: $113   ☐ Institutional: $333

Call 888-378-2537 or see mailing and pricing instructions below.
Online subscriptions are available at www.onlinelibrary.wiley.com

ORDER TOTALS:

Issue / Subscription Amount: $ _____

Shipping Amount: $ _____
(for single issues only – subscription prices include shipping)

Total Amount: $ _____

SHIPPING CHARGES:
First Item $5.00
Each Add'l Item $3.00

(No sales tax for U.S. subscriptions. Canadian residents, add GST for subscription orders. Individual rate subscriptions must
be paid by personal check or credit card. Individual rate subscriptions may not be resold as library copies.)

BILLING & SHIPPING INFORMATION:

☐ **PAYMENT ENCLOSED:** *(U.S. check or money order only. All payments must be in U.S. dollars.)*

☐ **CREDIT CARD:** ☐ VISA ☐ MC ☐ AMEX

Card number _____ Exp. Date _____

Card Holder Name _____ Card Issue # _____

Signature _____ Day Phone _____

☐ **BILL ME:** *(U.S. institutional orders only. Purchase order required.)*

Purchase order # _____
Federal Tax ID 13559302 • GST 89102-8052

Name _____

Address _____

Phone _____ E-mail _____

Copy or detach page and send to: **John Wiley & Sons, PTSC, 5th Floor**
989 Market Street, San Francisco, CA 94103-1741

Order Form can also be faxed to: **888-481-2665**

PROMO JBNND